The Tyranny of Science

The Tyranny of Science

Paul Feyerabend

Edited, and with an Introduction, by Eric Oberheim

polity

First published in Italian as *Ambiguità e armonia: lezioni trentine*
© Gius. Laterza e Figli, 1996.
Published by arrangement with Marco Vigevani Agenzia Letteraria.

This English edition © Polity Press, 2011

Polity Press
65 Bridge Street
Cambridge CB2 1UR, UK

Polity Press
350 Main Street
Malden, MA 02148, USA

ISBN-13: 978-0-7456-5189-7 (hardback)
ISBN-13: 978-0-7456-5190-3 (paperback)

A catalogue record for this book is available from the British Library.

Typeset in 11 on 13 pt Sabon
by Toppan Best-set Premedia Limited
Printed and bound in Great Britain by MPG Books Group Ltd, Bodmin, Cornwall

The publisher has used its best endeavours to ensure that the URLs for external websites referred to in this book are correct and active at the time of going to press. However, the publisher has no responsibility for the websites and can make no guarantee that a site will remain live or that the content is or will remain appropriate.

Every effort has been made to trace all copyright holders, but if any have been inadvertently overlooked the publisher will be pleased to include any necessary credits in any subsequent reprint or edition.

For further information on Polity, visit our website:
www.politybooks.com

Contents

Editor's Acknowledgements

Thanks to Paul Hoyningen-Huene and Olaf Müller for supporting my research on Paul Feyerabend's philosophy which made this project possible, and to Gonzalo Munévar for his enthusiastic encouragement to edit and publish the manuscript. Also, thanks to Brigitte Parakenings for her invaluable work at the *Philosophisches Archiv, Universität Konstanz*, Germany, and in particular for providing copies of the videos. Marcel Weber, Helmut Heit, Daniel Sirtes, Matteo Collodel, Jeu-Jenq Yuann and Vitali Filipov all contributed to the development of my understanding of Feyerabend's philosophy, for which I am grateful. Thanks to Johannes Binder, Simon Sharma and Kati Hennig for helping transform the typescript into this edition. My special thanks to Grazia Borrini-Feyerabend for her trust and guidance.

Editor's Introduction

Eric Oberheim

The sciences have unprecedented power to shape every aspect of our world. Such power comes with great responsibilities. Understanding what science is, how it works, and how it affects our lives is something that concerns us all. Paul Feyerabend (1924–94) devoted his life to tackling these issues. *The Tyranny of Science* is a series of five lectures originally entitled 'What is knowledge? What is science?' that Feyerabend gave to a general audience in 1992.[1] They are a condensed version of the lecture course he continuously redeveloped while teaching at Berkeley from 1958 to 1990.[2] As always, Feyerabend does not preach solutions, but challenges widespread preconceptions. He offers the critical tools that people need to form their own opinions about the ethical responsibilities of becoming a scientist. This book presents his final word in the last phase of his ever-changing views.

With *The Tyranny of Science,* Feyerabend masterfully interweaves the main elements of his philosophy into a story about the rise of Western rationalism and the entrenchment of a mythical, and yet oppressive, scientific world view. He attempts to identify the human costs of theoretical approaches to real problems. He raises concerns, challenging unfounded presuppositions about the sciences and how they affect society and the lives of individuals. And as awareness of these issues has steadily increased, these problems have become even more pressing. Like most of Feyerabend's previous productions, *The Tyranny of Science* is likely to provoke a wide range of sometimes even opposing reactions.[3]

To many, Paul Feyerabend will need no introduction. For others, the most that can be offered is a selective abstraction of such a complex and contentious figure. Feyerabend meant so many different things to so many different people that it is difficult, if not impossible, to place him squarely in any single tradition. Over an exceptionally dynamic career, he challenged many dogmas in philosophy and about science. His ideas and arguments are often ingenious and intriguing, but they are very hard to pin down. Indeed, a remarkable feature of Feyerabend's work is just how directly engaged he was with so many major developments in twentieth-century philosophy and the study of science; how he repeatedly reshaped his ideas at the forefront of current trends and changing interests.

After the Second World War, he studied history, physics and philosophy in Vienna, initially adopting the positivist attitude that empirical science is the basis of all knowledge; the rest either logic or just nonsense.[4] But in his doctoral thesis (1951), he attacked the foundations of that tradition, arguing against naive characterizations of the role of observation in experiment.[5] Later that year, he took a seminar with Niels Bohr, and then tried to identify and challenge dogmatic elements of the so-called 'Copenhagen Interpretation' of quantum mechanics.[6] He met Ludwig Wittgenstein and tried to rewrite the aphorisms of the *Philosophical Investigations* as a systematic argument, complaining of its dogmatic conception of philosophy as merely therapeutic.[7] He worked for Karl Popper in London, and carried critical rationalist ideas across Europe and North America, before becoming one of Popper's most vocal critics.[8] His most influential early paper, 'Explanation, Reduction and Empiricism' (1962) is about the controversial idea of the incommensurability of scientific theories. Nineteen sixty-two often serves as a landmark in the historical turn in the philosophy of science, closely linked to Thomas Kuhn and *The Structure of Scientific Revolutions.*[9] Since then, in many circles, the names Kuhn and Feyerabend often go hand-in-hand. But this overlooks Feyerabend's sharp criticism of the inherent dogmatisms in Kuhn's account of science, and his rejection of Kuhn's monistic phase-model in favour of his own pluralist account of scientific progress.[10] With the 'anything goes' and epistemological anarchism of *Against Method*, Feyerabend promoted methodological opportunism and pluralism in philosophy.[11] Ever since, Feyerabend has had the reputation of being an anti-science philosopher, even one of science's 'worst enemies'.[12] His developing views on science and society continue to be controversial.[13] Drawing on lessons he learned in Berkeley after the universities opened their doors to minorities, Feyerabend eventually even briefly dabbled in relativism,[14] before again rejecting it outright in favour of the more post-modernist approach to science recognized in his late philosophy.[15]

Like Woody Allen's *Zelig*, Feyerabend seemed to adapt himself to his changing environment, always engaging directly with the interests of his times – even often arguing both sides of the same issues. He tried to challenge dogmatic assumptions wherever he found them, pushing ideas to their extremes, challenging his reader to try to look outside the box. He was considered to be a maverick, an iconoclast, even some sort of living legend. His perpetual change of position, combined with his pointed rhetoric and excessive use of immanent criticism, often fuelled misinterpretation of his philosophy. Indeed, individual aspects of it were all too often misused by those who would exchange one tyranny for another,[16] instead of to protect progress from the stagnate oppression of dogmatic ideologies.

This was all part and parcel of Feyerabend's often misunderstood philosophical pluralism, which abstains from allegiance to any single point of view, and develops many different approaches to complex issues. He argued that while unanimity of opinion 'may be fitting for a church, for the frightened victims of some (ancient, or modern) myth, for the weak and willing followers of some tyrant; variety of opinion is a feature necessary for objective knowledge; and a method that encourages variety is also the only method that is compatible with a humanitarian outlook.'[17] One lesson he increasingly stressed was the danger of losing one's intellectual autonomy. To be convinced that one perspective delivers the truth is to be blinded to the truths offered by others, and belief in some truth is too often the motivation behind some oppression. And this holds for philosophy as well as politics. With typical Feyerabendian flair, he reverses a standard conception of the relation between truth and morality.[18] For Feyerabend, ethical decisions are not grounded in theoretical truths. Rather, methodological norms about the existence of truth and its utility are based on ethical decisions: 'the procedure leading to the adoption of a philosophical position cannot be *proof* . . . but must be a *decision* on the basis of preferences . . . Philosophers have habitually judged the situation in a very different manner. For them, only *one* of the many existing positions was true and therefore, possible. This attitude, of course, considerably restricts the domain of responsible choice.' He concludes 'ethics is, therefore, the basis of everything else.'[19]

His approach to knowledge and epistemology tries explicitly to take something positive from every experience. He draws from a great variety of sources, arguing that there is no idea, however ancient or absurd, that is incapable of contributing to the improvement of knowledge.[20] He insisted that developing divergent points of view promotes progress better than sticking to just one perspective, no matter how successful it may seem. On this account, scientific progress is not some linear progression towards truth, or a process that converges towards an ideal view. It is rather an ever *'expanding ocean of alternatives'*, each of which forces the others into greater articulation; all of them contributing through the process of competition to the development of our understanding.[21]

Moreover, Feyerabend's pluralism was not merely theoretical.[22] He practised pluralism in philosophy, using many different methods, including linguistic analyses, *reductio ad absurdum*, historical investigation, images, dialogues, acting and just plain stories in order to develop his ideas. He even incorporated his life-long interest in theatre and performance directly into his philosophy, both theoretically and practically,[23] trying to combine science with art.[24] Feyerabend practised philosophical pluralism in the pursuit of progress and for the protection from the oppression of conservative ideas. His pluralistic approach to philosophy complements his understanding of the sciences, given both the disunity of science and the abundance of nature. He supported pluralism and opportunism in appreciation of this two-fold variety.

Just as *Against Method* is a collage of Feyerabend's early papers, *The Tyranny of Science* intertwines many themes from different phases in Feyerabend's philosophical development, even from early publications. It is not a systematic investigation. It is about the drawbacks of systematization. Feyerabend argues that some very basic and widespread assumptions about 'science' are simply false, and that substantial parts of scientific ideology were created on the basis of rather superficial generalizations that lead to absurd misconceptions of the nature of human life. He argues that far from solving the pressing problems of our age, such as war and poverty, scientific theorizing glorifies ephemeral generalities instead of confronting the real particulars that make life worth living. For the objectivity and universality of science are based on abstraction, and as such, they come at a high cost. Abstraction drives a wedge between our thoughts and our experience, resulting in the degeneration of both. Theoreticians, as opposed to practitioners, tend to impose tyranny through the concepts they use, which abstract away from the subjective experiences that make life meaningful.

In Feyerabend's story, 'science', 'scientific reason', 'the scientific world view' are all explicitly just a public relations myth that is part of the problem he is addressing. Science does not speak in a single voice, and does not offer a single coherent world view. In fact, it is the very myth that scientific truth can serve as an adequate guide to a subjectively meaningful reality that Feyerabend strives to expose. And it is the inhumane consequences of a society that succumbs to the seduction of the theoretical that Feyerabend strives to indict. The various sciences (not 'science') can and do use theory to tackle pressing problems. So the sciences, in themselves, are not the enemy. They play their part in real solutions. But in our current society, becoming a scientist can take its toll. For scientists learn to be objective, to approach the world as an abstraction. Instead of experiencing what the world has to offer and using science to help people, the current system encourages treating problems theoretically, real situations as mere possibilities, even people as objects. That is the source of the problem to which Feyerabend calls our attention in *The Tyranny of Science*. It is Feyerabend at his best, both provocative and captivating, as he challenges some modern myths about science.

The Tyranny of Science
Paul Feyerabend

1

Conflict and Harmony

You may have heard or read in a newspaper that recently cosmologists have become very excited. Let me explain to you why. One of the prevalent theories in cosmology today is the Big Bang. According to this theory the universe started about fifteen billion years ago from a tiny ball of energy. The ball expanded until it reached its present size. Various things were supposed to have happened during the first 300,000 years of the expansion. Gamov, for example, conjectured that during that period the density of radiation greatly exceeded the density of matter, that the radiation cooled during the expansion and survived until today.[1] Nothing was found and the conjecture was forgotten. Then, about twenty years ago, some radioastronomers were disturbed by a constant noise they could not eliminate. It was independent of the location of the sun, of planets, of galaxies or galactic clusters; in other words, it was isotropic. In fact, it had all the properties of the background radiation predicted by Gamov. This was a great triumph for the Big Bang view, until some people realized, again on the basis of purely theoretical considerations, that the radiation should not have been isotropic. After all, the universe was already quite lumpy when it arose and the lumps should have shown in the radiation. They were not. Many astronomers who did not like the Big

Bang regarded this as a major difficulty. Now, just two or three weeks ago, changes of the right order of magnitude were found by means of a satellite especially designed for that purpose.[2] This was really miraculous. Just think of it! We are talking about a situation far beyond anything we can realize in our laboratories. What we have are a few observations, some extrapolations, laws of matter are inferred from evidence gained in a space–time region vanishingly small when compared with the total history of the universe and are then applied in extreme conditions of a mostly theoretical kind. There are a few scattered observations and predictions and – lo and behold! – everything hangs together beautifully.

Is it surprising that the defenders of the Big Bang who had often been criticized for their weird and pseudotheological assumptions were elated? That they regarded the confirmation as an important event, not only for themselves, but for all of humanity? People were always interested in things they could not see and they invented fantastic stories to explain the world and the course of their lives. They spoke of divine beings, of monsters terrible to behold; they spoke of chaos and of battles that shook the entire universe. A few observations sufficed to uphold a rich and complex scenario. Cosmology is exactly like that – this is why so many people are interested in it. Anyhow, astrophysicists, cosmologists, laypersons, theologians in search of interdisciplinary convergences – all these people got very excited by the discovery I have described.

Now, forget astrophysics and consider some other things that are happening in our world. Remember the riots in Los Angeles? About a month ago, a black motorist was stopped by the Los Angeles police and severely beaten. A bystander with a video camera filmed the affair and sent the tape to a TV station. For a few days every TV station in the country and many stations abroad showed the tape. It was a pretty gruesome affair – maybe you saw it, too. The policemen were identified and temporarily suspended. Then came the trial. The conclusion was that with one exception all policemen had done their job properly and were innocent of any crime. Now the ghettos exploded – in Los Angeles, San Francisco, Baltimore – surprisingly, not in Chicago. Forty-four people were killed in L. A. alone, thousands were wounded, stores were demolished, entire blocks burned down – unfortunately mostly in the poorer sections. Finding himself in an election year, even the President remarked that, maybe, the policemen ought to have been punished.[3]

Think next of the events in Yugoslavia.[4] About two months ago, a student of sociology from Yugoslavia sent me a tape and a letter. The tape shows what by now has become commonplace: destruction of houses, of entire cities, killings, mutilations of the most inhuman kind. He had always believed in the power of democracy and free speech, he said in the letter; he had believed that conflicts could be solved by a rational debate – and so on. 'Now I only trust a man with a gun who is on my side.' And, indeed, he is right. For who can reason with torturers, murderers and rapists? Who can reason with an all-consuming hatred that turns human beings into killing machines? There were wonderful exceptions – for example a young couple, he a Muslim, she an orthodox Christian. They loved each other and they married in public to show that religious differences were no obstacle to love and understanding. But these are exceptions. The rest of us – and the events of the Nazi period show that this includes intellectuals and the so-called 'educated people' – seem to be only steps away from bestiality.[5]

Now, compare the two kinds of events I have just described. On the one side there is a great and exciting discovery, affecting, so it seems, all of humankind. On the other side war, murder, cruelty. Is there a connection? Is there a way of making sense of both? Is there a way of using the products of our curiosity and our intelligence to influence, attenuate, redirect our base instincts? Or do we have to concede that history is a crazy quilt of happenings which have nothing in common and that human nature is kind of a shopping bag containing disparate commodities, some divine, others monstrous with no connection between them?

5

Conflict and Harmony

It seems that disconnectedness is indeed a major characteristic of our civilization and perhaps even of our age. There is something called 'science'. It claims to deal with the details and the overall structure of the world. It tries to explain how matter came into existence, how life arose and when, and in what manner human beings arrived on this Earth. Science seems to be about all there is. But science is quite exclusive. Let me read to you what Jacques Monod, a molecular biologist, a political activist and a Nobel Prize Winner said about the scientific world view.[6] 'Cold and austere' he wrote:

> proposing no explanation but imposing an ascetic renunciation of all other spiritual fare [the idea that objective knowledge is the only authentic source of truth] was not of a kind to allay anxiety but aggravated it instead. By a single stroke it claimed to sweep away the tradition of a hundred thousand years, which had become one with human nature itself. It wrote an end to the ancient animist covenant between man and nature, leaving nothing in place of that precious bond but an anxious quest in a frozen universe of solitude. With nothing to recommend it but a certain puritan arrogance, how could such an idea win acceptance? It did not; it still has not. It has however commanded recognition; but that is because, solely because of its prodigious power of performance.
>
> (*Chance and Necessity*, New York 1972, p. 170)

Science informs and performs, says Monod. It not only does not deal with meanings, it intentionally removes everything that is only vaguely related to them. The result is that 'the more we know about the universe, the more pointless it seems' as Steven Weinberg wrote.[7]

Well, you will say, giving hope and providing meaning is not the task of science, it is the task of religion. So, let us turn to this area.

It is true that religion talks about the soul and aims and meanings. Not only that – religion also creates meaning in places that at first sight seem to be devoid of it. But today and in the West the application of religious ideas and rituals

6

is strictly limited. The believer is divided into a part that acts 'as a scientist' and another part that acts, say, 'as a Christian'. 'As a scientist' (s)he renounces faith and revelation and keeps away from meanings. 'As a Christian' (s)he relies on faith and follows divine patterns. There exists no way of infusing science itself with a religious spirit. Religion is something that is added after science has done its work; it is not part of this work. Secondly, I am not so sure that making religion part of science would be an advantage. Scientists are already much too self-righteous. Besides, Christians, to take just one example, have not been the best of people. They maligned the Jews, humiliated women and killed hundreds of thousands in the name of the faith. Maybe it is better to be a cold, unmoved and 'objective' collector of facts than a passionate killer. Thirdly, religion is not one thing, it is many. There are Buddhists, Muslims, Quakers, snake worshippers and each one of these groups is further subdivided into more tolerant and more aggressive factions. A religion that appeals to all people and all professions and that appeals to their love, not to their self-righteousness and their murderous instincts, has yet to be found.

Next, there are the 'arts'. Today, many scientists want to make us believe that scientific research is not as tight-assed as the Monod quotation seems to indicate. There is an artistic spirit, they say, there is 'creativity', 'imagination', there are metaphors, analogies, 'aesthetic dimensions' – and so on. Moreover there are now scientific theories that seem to be applicable both to matter and to the movements of the spirit. All this sounds very nice but has little influence on the day-to-day practice and the institutional ramifications of research. Where is the research team that gets a prize for its aesthetic achievements? Where is the journal that accepts articles because of the creative insights they contain? Wolfgang Pauli was an outstanding physicist and a Nobel Prize Winner.[8] He deplored the modern separation of science and religion but he kept most of these ideas to himself – for fear of being ridiculed. Besides, who is this creature 'art', whom scientists are now wooing with such abandon? What is it that links, say, the cupola of the Florence Cathedral to Jackson Pollock's urinations, rather than to Galileo's mechanical studies? As in religion we have a wide variety of products held together, rather artificially (or should I say 'artistically'?) by a single name. In a way this is true even of the sciences. The general theory of relativity is science – but so is botany. Botany is based on a careful inspection of objects one can see and hold in one's hand, while the general theory of relativity uses daring generalizations about inaccessibles. Remember the Big Bang? Everybody agrees that it is many orders of magnitude removed from known physical conditions – and yet the laws we found to hold under these conditions are supposed to apply to it as well. Or compare elementary particle physics with economics. The one is successful, the other a rather doubtful affair. The one is checked by experiment, the other by trends one cannot easily identify or control. Every field has empiricists who want science to stay close to the facts and dreamers who don't mind when their speculations clash with well-established experimental results. Even special subjects such as sociology or hydrodynamics are divided into schools with different methodologies. So, what we get when looking around are grand subdivisions between areas which are themselves discordant collections of methods and results; all this prefaced by the caveat: do not mix approaches!

Well, there is still philosophy. Philosophy, it seems, is a discipline that provides an overview and puts things in perspective. At least this is how it started in the West. The early Greek philosophers were cultural critics. They looked at what they found, condemned some things and applauded and modified others. Plato, for example, criticized painting, tragedy and the epic for appealing to the emotions, telling lies and generally confusing people. Later philosophers produced entire systems. These systems contained all that had been achieved, but carefully arranged according to the insights of their creators. Like scientists, artists and religious reformers philosophers have by now accumulated a rather disorganized heap of opinions and approaches. There are Kantians, Hegelians, Heideggerians; there are Kuhnians,

Popperians, Wittgensteinians; there are the followers of Foucault, Derrida, Ricoeur; there are neoaristotelians, neothomists – I could go on forever. Most of these philosophies started as attempts to put an end to the battle of the schools. They did not succeed. The attempts soon became schools themselves and joined the battle. Besides, much that is now being written in philosophy is rather trivial and without wider interest. One philosopher creates a new fashion and a whole herd starts investigating who does and who does not belong to it (*Traces of Postmodernism in Franco Labbroculo's Early Work* is not at all an untypical title). So, disconnection is the rule and harmony not just the exception – it simply does not exist.

But is this really a disadvantage? Is it really a disadvantage that there are many different areas of research which are run by people with different interests and produce widely differing results? Supermarkets are rather convenient. They not only provide you with an abundance of products, they also show you things you did not know but could have used. What the sciences and the humanities, what religion and the arts are offering are spiritual supermarkets, as it were, with different departments and many connections between them. Consider also that individuals differ in their inclinations, beliefs, convictions; that there are different cultures and that each culture evolved through occasionally conflicting stages. Each culture provides material, social and spiritual guidance for its members starting from birth through maturity to the grave. The guidance is mediated by individuals and these have widely different characters and opinions. Still, there are certain general regularities which characterize them as belonging to one culture rather than to another.

Now cultures and individuals already have ways of dealing with the problems that might arise in their realm. If, using these ways, they sever connections between enterprises such as science and religion, subjects such as physics and sociology or cultures such as early nineteenth-century Japanese culture and the West, then this is their business. Moaning about a 'lack of harmony' means condemning arrangements that have grown over millennia. And those who are speaking of harmony sound suspiciously like tyrants, who want to subject any variety they find to their own harmonious rule. True, there is hunger and strife in this world and there are amazing discoveries. But why should everybody react to them in the same way and, more importantly, why should both find a place in a single coherent scheme?

Because, you might answer, they occur in a single coherent world. Scientists live in this world; so do warlords and their victims. Besides, scientists, warlords, the hungry and the rich – they all are human beings. If we want to understand what is going on and if we want to change what displeases us then we have to know the nature both of the world and of human beings and we also have to know how they fit together. Only a comprehensive theory, only a world view can give us this information. This is how some writers, the divine Plato among them, have justified the need for a coherent account of everything there is. Most people, scientists and prophets included, would agree. There is one world, we all live in it, so we had better learn how things hang together.

But with this assumption, unfortunately, we are back where we started from. First of all – whom shall we choose as our teachers? Many individuals, groups, schools compete for that position.

Secondly, who says that the parts of the world hang together in a harmonious way? That strife is absent from the world at large? For the Gnostics the world was split into two; there was the world of God and the world of matter created by low-level demons. A human being, the Gnostic said, contains elements from both worlds. (S)he has an immortal soul and a decaying body – (s)he is, in the words of some Gnostics, a speck of gold embedded in dirt. Conflict is built right into her/his nature. The more (s)he knows about matter, the farther away (s)he is from her/his real being. Translated into later terminology this means that the sciences of matter and the sciences of the spirit are not only different, but must be kept separate – otherwise they do not correctly represent reality. Strictly speaking there cannot and should not be any science of matter – this is too foul and too decep-tive a subject to even think about. A later medieval saying gives us a flavour of what this implies for the human body: *Intra faeces et urinam nascimur* – we are born between shit and piss. Note, incidentally, that some scientists, Planck[9] and Einstein among them, held very similar views: there is an 'objective reality' which is eternal and stable. It is entirely material (here the scientists differ from the Gnostics). On the other side there are the day-to-day lives of human beings – their birth, their growth and development, their joys and sorrows and, finally, their death. These lives are an 'illusion' (Einstein's word). They do not count when compared with 'reality'. But while the Gnostics admitted that given such a world it needed revelation to gain knowledge, our scientists believe that they can somehow reason their way from illusion to reality. They are Gnostics, yes, but rather confused ones. At any rate, the idea of a harmonious world to which we all belong is one idea among many. It cannot serve as a measure for the rest.

But even if the world were one, it is not at all certain that a world view would be the best guide through it. World views are not only incomplete, they also deceive and, to use a somewhat bloated phrase, they diminish our humanity. They suggest that plans for improvement can and perhaps even should neglect personal matters and details, and attend to pervasive trends only. But what if there are no such trends and if what we believe are trends are just the projections of our own limits? And what about those ingredients of our humanity, what about compassion, love and personal under-standing, which are mobilized only by the sight of a human face and which die when confronted with generalities? I know there are people who think they can love HUMANITY and who even write about this strange love affair. But their love quickly evaporates when you present them with particu-lar faces attached to particular bodies exuding a particular and perhaps penetrating smell. Besides, a love for humanity has never prevented anyone from being cruel to individuals that seem to endanger it. Guidance by abstract ideas is a dangerous business when not controlled by strong personal relations. There is no way around it: Reacting to the world is a personal (family, group) matter that cannot be replaced by even the most enchanting world view.

Does this mean that there is nothing further to be said? Certainly not! Individuals, families, groups and cultures react to their surroundings. They are what they are today because of the experiences, ideas, shocks, etc. that they had in their past. There is no reason why we, and this means you and I and many other people, should not in our own way contribute to these surroundings, experiences and shocks by means of books, speeches, theatrical productions, financial contributions and compositions, or simply by having a few affairs with the men and/or women of the 'other side'. Now, we are here sitting in the lecture hall of a university and I assume that you have come to hear ideas rather than see a demonstration of sexual perversities. So, ideas you are going to get – but in a special way!

First of all I shall not give you a 'systematic' presentation. A systematic presentation removes ideas from the ground that made them grow and arranges them in an artificial pattern. If the pattern pleases influential people they will write books about it, make it required reading in their university courses, arrange their examinations accordingly, and very soon the pattern will appear to be reality itself. People who do not know it, but hear about it, will suspect that they are missing something. Popular writers will explain it in simple terms, movies will celebrate the heroes who invented it, and icons of all shapes and sizes will remind the *hoi polloi* how little they really know and how much they have to learn.[10]

Well, to be honest, this kind of procedure does not impress me at all. The process is very interesting; it shows to what extent fashions rule the 'world of the spirit' (to use another bloated expression). But the starting point – the 'systematic presentation' leaves me cold. What I am interested in is how, under what circumstances and in what personal ways, people acquired a liking for certain patterns. Why, for example, do so many people believe in a reality that not only remains unmoved by their actions but controls every detail of their behaviour? How did this idea arise and why did people fall for it? Trying to find an answer to questions such as these, I am also trying to find situations which I can understand, emotionally as well as intellectually; situations which involve my entire being (to use still another bloated phrase) and not only a few well-trained, i.e. half dead, cells of my brain. But how do I find such situations?

Well, there are many ways. One of them is to present ideas and world views historically, i.e. to tell how they arose and why people accepted them and acted accordingly. This is by no means a simple matter for the way we see history is influenced by the patterns that have been hypnotizing us. Moreover, I am not a scholar. I know a little scandal here, a little idea there, and out of that I construct my stories. Strictly speaking my lectures will be fairytales woven around events that are vaguely historical. That does not really worry me for I have the suspicion that real scholars also tell fairytales, only their fairytales are longer and much more complicated – which does not mean that they cannot be very interesting. Hearing mere fairytales may not be your cup of tea – you may want to hear THE TRUTH. Well, if that's what you want, then you are better off elsewhere – only for the life of me, I can't tell you exactly where that would be.

My fairytale starts with a question: was there ever a connection between the majestic events in the heavens and the sad and often silly events on the Earth? Remember, that is how I started my lecture: new evidence for the Big Bang on the one side, war and misery on the other. What is the connection? The answer is that many periods and many cultures took a connection for granted. Homer, for example, combines human actions and divine actions into a single and rather dramatic story. The twists and turns of the Trojan wars, the troubles of Odysseus and many other events were not accidents; nor were they caused by humans entirely; they were also influenced by the gods, who quarrelled with each other and had their own ideas about how the world should be run.

I know – to many so-called agnostics this story sounds rather silly; who is going to take it seriously? Well, the story was taken seriously by some of the most intelligent people of antiquity. And they had excellent reasons. For them the gods were not just hypothetical entities like quarks or super-strings; they were a living presence that permeated their lives and the lives of everybody around them. Their presence could be felt in woods, on mountains, on the shore, at home, during waking time and in the course of dreams. Feeling very angry, you might feel that an alien force had taken possession of you and you might give a name to this force – the name of a god. The Homeric epics, where events such as these occur, played an enormous role in Greek education. This was the basic educational text even in democratic Athens and as late as the fifth century BC. It told the Greeks about their history, their gods, about the nature of virtue and the shape of the world.

Now comes the second part of my fairytale: the role of philosophers. I said 'philosophers' – but the people I have in mind differed in many aspects from our professors. Thales, for example, who is often called the first philosopher, was one of the leading citizens of Miletus, an important harbour on the western coast of Asia Minor. He gave political advice to his fellow citizens, seemed to know astronomy, made a killing on the olive-press market, and occasionally acted as an engineer. Mind you, we have no direct evidence of these events; all we have are rumours which may have started during Thales' lifetime but which we know from reports about two generations later. Plato, for example, tells us the following story: Walking with his eyes glued to the stars, Thales fell into a ditch. A peasant girl standing nearby mocked him: 'Good old Thales!' she exclaimed; 'You may be at home in the sky, but you sure don't know what's in front of your nose!' To rescue Thales from such ridicule, Aristotle told the entirely different story of the olive presses. Now Aristotle was already a fully fledged philosopher, the first philosophy professor in fact, and so he added that Thales entered business not because he wanted to get rich but in order to show that philosophers could win in any profession, provided they choose to enter it; in most cases they just weren't interested.

Other stories are about more 'theoretical' achievements. For example, Thales is supposed to have measured the height of a pyramid by measuring the length of its shadow when the shadow of a stick was as long as the stick itself. And he is supposed to have demonstrated that the sum of angles in a triangle was equal to the 'straight angle', or to 180 degrees, as we would say today. He may have used the figure below.

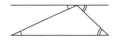

But if he did, then his 'proof' was not a sequence of logically connected statements, but simply a picture. The picture showed what was the case. The picture itself was the proof.

In sum, Thales seems to have been an all-round intelligent individual who touched the imagination of later generations and was revered for his achievements: He was one of the Seven Wise Men of Antiquity.

According to some reports, Thales also said that everything was made of water and that everything was full of gods. These two assertions became his passport into the history of philosophy. Aristotle, who introduced a general notion of substance, regarded him as a (rather simple-minded materialistic) predecessor. Thales, he said, assumed just one substance, and it was water. Later historians of philosophy took it from there. Guthrie's six-volume *History of Ancient Philosophy* still has a special chapter on Thales.[11]

The first assertion was rather plausible for the Greeks, who, according to the Platonic Socrates, 'lived around the Mediterranean like frogs around a pond'. They saw how water turned into mist, rose, dissolved into air, formed clouds, turned into water again and could be solid like ice. Water gave warmth, and took warmth away. It could be any one of the four traditional elements, water, fire, air and earth. Besides, it was needed for life; it sustained life even in the desert which lacked its fluid form. Making assumptions such as these, Thales anticipated a basic principle of modern science – that there is a unity behind the variety of appearances.

The second assumption – everything is full of gods – is ambiguous. Thales may have wanted to widen the traditional view of divinities, or he may have made fun of it: Gods are not just on Olympus and they are not merely concerned with the fate of Trojan warriors; they act everywhere, according to fixed principles and thus can be replaced by these. Thales' criticism – if it was a criticism – does not seem to have been very harsh. His successors were much less polite.

Let me introduce you to Xenophanes. Thales dabbled in many fields, knew lots of things, but he was not an expert. Xenophanes was an expert, a reciter of poetry, to be more precise. This was a well-established profession. Reciters or rhapsodies could be found in every city. They were invited to parties, contributed to the entertainment and challenged other reciters to contests: One would quote a few lines of an obscure poem and the other had to continue. Xenophanes has left a vivid account of his travels 'up and down the shore of the Mediterranean' and of the parties he attended.

These professionals were not only entertainers, they also educated their audience. They explained obscure passages and clarified the background; they knew the gods, their functions and their deeds; they could tell events from the history of the cities they had visited and talk entertainingly about the customs of strange countries; they kept alive the memory of heroes and wise men. They instructed their listeners in the virtues and had examples of how easily virtue deteriorated into vice. Homer was their main source; experience was another. Occasionally they added lines and stories of their own. And it is quite possible that they started criticizing their material. At any rate, that is what Xenophanes did.

'You', he said, criticizing the Pythagoreans (who believed that the soul of a person who had just died might next turn up in an animal, a dog for example) – 'you stranger, stop beating that dog! That is my departed friend howling!' Or about the Homeric view of the gods: 'All their vices the humans have ascribed to the gods – but if cows and horses had hands, just like humans, and if they could draw, then surely they would draw cows and horses as their god' – and so on.

Incidentally, I do not quote verbatim, not even in translation. I quote just the sense and the style from memory. On that occasion, let me tell you a little about the evidence. What do we know about these ancient thinkers? Do we have their writings? How do we know what they said? Well, the situation is rather interesting. Most of the evidence consists of manuscripts that were written, i.e. copied, from other manuscripts more than a thousand years after the event. The first manuscripts containing Platonic writings, for example, come from the eleventh century AD – and Plato lived in the fifth/fourth century BC! True, there are scraps of papyri, but they are short and contain only small parts of the text. So, one problem about, let us say, Plato is: Are the manuscripts reliable? Do they really contain what Plato has written, or has the name of Plato been attached to the text of a different author to give it authority? Another problem is the language. Plato wrote Greek. But like every great author he used it in an idiosyncratic way – he gave new meanings to some terms, new shades of meaning to others, and we have to guess what he intended. Naturally, different translators make different guesses. Just try the following experiment. Take one of Plato's dialogues, start reading it until you come to a passage that is difficult to understand and then compare different translations of that passage. You will be amazed!

However, Plato is a 'simple' case compared with, say, Thales, or Anaxagoras. Plato founded a school, the Academy, which lasted into the fifteenth century. The academy took care that the Platonic writings were kept in good order. There was no academy around Thales. Aristotle, who lived only three generations after him, reports from rumours about Thales, not from Thales, and he uses his own terminology, not Thales' words. We have bits and pieces from the other pre-Socratic philosophers, mostly in writings of the Church Fathers, who wanted to compare Christianity with what had gone on before. Therefore, be really sceptical when you hear a guy, for example me, saying: 'Anaximander asserted that. . . .' After all, all we know from Anaximander himself is one sentence – and a very puzzling sentence it is! In the case of Xenophanes we are a little better off. We have long stretches of his poems which were preserved by Athenaeus because of the hints they contain about the eating habits at the parties Xenophanes attended. And Athenaeus was interested in eating habits.

So, back to Xenophanes!

Xenophanes not only mocked traditional religious views, he also had ideas of his own. He assumed that there was only one divine being. It, or rather He (naturally, it was a He), was Pure Thought. No feelings, no compassion, certainly no sense of humour. To make up for it, He was Super Powerful. He was also very lazy, 'He does not go up and down but by the power of this thought moves all there is' says Xenophanes. Not an individual I would be interested in meeting. It is different with most intellectuals. They wet their pants with excitement when reading about this magnificent creature. 'What a sublime conception of divinity' is a typical remark. 'Sublime'? – my foot. I prefer Athena, or Hermes, or Aphrodite. The great advantage seems to be that Xenophanes' monster is no longer 'anthropomorphic' – it has no human features. In other words, it is inhuman. I cannot for the life of me understand why that should be an advantage. Why should a universe guided by an alien be preferable to a universe populated by familiar figures? Besides, human properties were not entirely removed. They still exist, but in isolation and monstrously enlarged. 'All thought'. If the gods are supposed to be 'far from human', then why should they still be able to think? At any rate, human affairs and divine affairs, or human lives and the rest of the world, now have very little to do with each other: The disconnectedness I discussed in the beginning starts insinuating itself. Later philosophers, Parmenides especially, went much further. They explicitly asserted that compared with Being (Being, in Parmenides, replaces Xenophanes' monster) human existence is a chimera.

Now the interesting thing is the way in which these views spread and eventually infected the whole world. First, they became popular among people with influence. These people did not always agree, but they studied the views, wrote reports, revised them and in this way created a 'tradition'. And as history for a long time was written by people with influence, the beginning of this tradition is now known as 'The Rise of Rationalism', as the 'Greek Revolution' or as the 'Greek Miracle', and it is thought to be something very important – the birth of Western civilization, no less. The development initiated by the tradition changed the life of intellectuals; it did not directly change the life of the common people. But the common people were slowly dragged into it, whether they wanted it or not. The peculiarities of science, its urge for 'objectivity' are all in some way connected to this distant 'Revolution' – just remember the passage I quoted from Monod! The world at large as seen by scientists is separated from the insignificant events on this planet and even humans, as seen by scientists (molecular biologists especially) are separated from what they experience themselves as being. To many writers it seems that this separation is not an accident, that it is not something we slid into unawares. They assume that it is the work of outstanding individuals who, trying to understand their surroundings, refined their ideas and methods and finally discovered the (inhuman) nature of reality.

However, there are lots of questions we can ask. Was it good that the ancient philosophers turned the traditional gods into Thought, Fire and unchanging blocks of Being? Was the change they recommended initiated by them or were they being swept along by forces that they did not notice and over which they had no control? If so, what were these forces? Can we free ourselves from their influence or can we bend them so that they serve our wishes? And, if the latter, what are our wishes? Should we support the consequences of this gradual petrification of life and welcome the insights that came with it or should we look for something better? Does it really matter what we think? Perhaps we are stuck with our age and can only hope that Fate will bring us a better future. Or is the presentation I gave mistaken, both historically and 'philosophically' (whatever that means). Lots of questions arise – and I have no intention of answering them. What I want to do here is to provide material for thought and confusion.

And there is plenty such material.

To start with, the historical period I am talking about did not only have philosophers; it also had poets, politicians, generals, public nuisances like Socrates and public speakers like Demosthenes, and much, much more. And there were the playwrights – Aeschylus, Sophocles, Euripides, Aristophanes, among others.

The theatre to which these writers contributed was very different from the theatre today. The production of tragedies and comedies was part of large religious festivals which had religious ceremonies side by side with athletic contests and shows of all sorts. Everybody was invited – as a matter of fact, everybody was supposed to come – and everybody did come; from the city, from the countryside with food for the day, for the theatrical performances lasted a long time. Each play was evaluated by judges who were under public pressure and whose judgement reflected the attitude of the audience. Plays were performed only once (there were very few exceptions). Usually they were written and produced by the same person who might also pay for the production. They were topical – many public figures were ridiculed in Aristophanes' comedies. The general outlines of most tragedies were well known, from Homer and from other poets. People knew what to expect. And they understood what the author intended when he deviated from the norm. They understood his 'message'. Occasionally they liked it; on other occasions the author was fined or otherwise punished for reminding people of painful events. Placed into the centre of a direct democracy, this institution was one of the best educational instruments that ever existed. It educated people by challenging them to think, not by beating them down, and it made them think by appealing to their senses and their feeling, not only to their brains. There is a report that Agatharchus, the stage manager of Aeschylus, introduced perspective. There is another report that people recoiled in fear when Aeschylus' furies entered the stage. Showbiz at its best. So what were these tragedies all about?

We have two general accounts of ancient tragedy, one critical, the other supportive. In Book X of his *Republic* Plato examines the 'imitative arts' as he called them. His conclusion is that they have no place in a perfect society. The leaders and the citizens of a perfect society need to know how things really are. But artists, painters for example, do not lead us towards reality, they befuddle us with appearances. An artisan makes beds and chairs. These are useful objects – one can lie in them or sit on them. Trying to make a good bed, an artisan has before himself the idea of a perfect bed. For Plato this idea, which is the standard for all good beds, is real. The bed made by the artisan is not as perfect as the perfect bed – it is a compromise between the perfect bed, the properties of matter which resists perfection, and the failings of the artisan. Still, it is useful and it is only one step removed from reality. Now take a painting of a bed. To start with, you cannot do anything with it. You cannot sit on it and you certainly cannot have a good night's sleep in it. It has no useful function. Moreover, it is the copy of a copy of a real thing which means it is twice removed from reality, a chimera, practically. The theatre has further disadvantages. It rouses the emotions. But emotions drown clear thought and clear thought is needed to create and maintain a good society. Besides, the theatre teaches the wrong kind of behaviour: People hit by misfortune whine and carry on instead of keeping a manly silence. Plato concludes that a good society must forbid the theatre, 'But', he adds, (again I paraphrase) 'having myself once been enchanted by poetry I invite those transported by her charms to defend her, in verse or in prose.'

Conflict and Harmony

Aristotle's *Poetics* is such a defence. We have only part of it – the section on comedy has been lost (and was found again in Eco's *The Name of the Rose*).[12] It was one of the most influential books in the history of the arts. It affected Corneille, Racine, Lessing (who corrected translation errors that had misled the French); Brecht wrote a little book against it,[13] Dürrenmatt admired it. Tragedy, according to Aristotle, is based on action, not on words alone; the action is supposed to have a tight structure – simple narration ('one damn thing after another') will not do. There must be a beginning, a middle and an end. Moreover, the events which form the action must be linked to each other – one event must with necessity lead to the next event, and to the next and, finally, to the tragic climax. Approaching the climax the audience experiences fear and pity. Moving away from it, it experiences a release of the emotions, a catharsis. Being built in this way tragedy has two functions. Through the structure of the plot it reveals what can and must happen; today we would say that it reveals social laws. This is why, according to Aristotle, poetry 'is more philosophical than history'; history only tells us what did in fact happen. The second function of tragedy is therapeutic, as some people would say. It reinforces the effect social laws have upon the human mind. In a way it is a brainwash procedure. By arousing strong negative emotions (fear and pity) and then releasing them it imprints what happened during the release. Initiation rites use different methods to create the negative emotions and their release and they add the message to be imprinted from the outside. According to Aristotle's description of tragedy it is the message itself that creates the emotions which then reinforce it. One cannot think of a better way to keep people committed to the society in which they live. But was this the way of the tragedians themselves? It was not.

To see this, let us look at a real tragedy, at a trilogy in fact, namely the *Oresteia* of Aeschylus. The basic story is that Agamemnon, the leader of the Greeks in Troy, was killed by his wife Clytemnestra and her lover Aegisthus. Not only that; to take all powers away from him, his limbs were separated from his body and tied around his neck. Through this act he was turned into a non-entity. Revenge alone could save his memory. Revenge was the task of his son, Orestes. This was an ancient law. To take revenge Orestes had to kill his mother, Clytemnestra. But killing his mother he would get into conflict with another law, which forbade the killing of blood relatives. Apollo ordered him to kill Clytemnestra. He did so and was persecuted by the Furies. He fled to the altar of Athena and here awaited his fate.

At this place let me make two comments. First, that the action reveals a contradiction inherent in the social laws of the time. The contradiction is found by an indirect argument: action A (not killing the murderers of his father) is forbidden, hence action non-A, i.e. killing the murderers of his father is required but equally forbidden. We have a paradox. The formal structure of this paradox is similar to the formal structure of later paradoxes such as Russell's paradox about the class of all classes that do not contain themselves as members. It also uses the same form of reasoning – from premise to impossibility back to the negation of the premise. This is a rather sophisticated form of argumentation which entered mathematics only later (some historians say that Parmenides was the prime mover).

My second comment is that this amazing abstract structure is embedded in and almost hidden by a complex net of events. For example, Agamemnon belonged to the cursed house of Atreus. His death may have been part of the curse. Would the curse last forever? Furthermore, Agamemnon had sacrificed Iphigenia, Clytemnestra's daughter, to placate the gods and he had betrayed Clytemnestra. She therefore had every reason to hate and to despise him. Personal, historical, social events and tendencies and an abstract structure are woven into a compelling and terrifying story about the fate of individuals, generations and entire cities.

To return to the play: Orestes, surrounded by the furies, is at Athena's altar waiting to have his case resolved one way or another. Athena arrives. She arranges a court hearing before a group of Athenian citizens. Note the role of this particular goddess: she does not herself decide the case; she supports an institution of the city that bears her name, presides at the meeting, but leaves the decision to its members. We are miles from Homer – and from Xenophanes' lazy god-monster. Athena questions Orestes, Apollo and the Furies. There comes a series of one liners which shows how arguments were conducted at the time: one party makes a statement which has a certain plausibility, the other party denies the statement using common sayings or well-known lines from poetry which are also plausible. What decides the case is the balance of the plausibility, not an abstract truth that is accessible to experts only. The question put before the jury is: Was Clytemnestra, Orestes' mother, a blood relative? The Furies say yes. Apollo says no: a mother is a breeding oven for the male seed which already contains the entire child. It emerges that Apollo's point of view is new – it is the new law of Zeus and it super-sedes the older law of the Furies. After the debate they have to vote; there is a majority of one in favour of the Furies. Athena adds her vote in favour of Orestes (she has been born, without a mother, from the forehead of Zeus) which means that Orestes goes free. The new law of Zeus seems to have triumphed – but no, says Athena to the Furies. You are part of the history of our city and you will continue to be part of its future. The new law does not replace you, it shares power with you, which means that from now on we shall regard you as a blessing, as the *Eumenides*, the well-meaning ones.

Well, it really does not make much sense to speak about a work like this in abstract terms. What you have to do is to read the trilogy, or even better, attend a performance that is directed not by a maniac who wants to get his name into print, but by a thoughtful producer who pays attention to all the elements of this rich tapestry, the personal, the institutional, the divine and the abstract. At any rate, Aeschylus has little to do with what either Plato or Aristotle or any other bloody philosopher says about tragedy. He is show business, political oratory, religious ceremony, *Fall of the*

House of Usher, biological debate, logical argumentation all in one.

Sophocles is different. In the *Oresteia* we have divine support for the institutions of the city. In Sophocles' *Antigone*, the gods continue playing their irrational games and the humans suffer as a consequence. Who is right? And how can we decide? There seems to be progress – but there is also much senseless suffering. Plato, in his dialogue *Eutyphron*, adds a further element. The story here is about a man who punished his slave by leaving him in a ditch. The slave died. The man did not mean for him to die – but that's what happened. The son of the man tells the authorities. They have a problem. How will they decide? One side believes that everything is in the hands of the gods. They say, 'According to the will of the gods'. The other side which reflects Plato's position assumes that the gods do not act arbitrarily, but in accordance with just laws. Now it is true that in Homer the gods are not the last authority. There is a higher power of a rather abstract kind. Plato articulates this power in a way that makes the gods superfluous. But this means that human suffering is no longer caused by a conflict that resides in the world itself. Human suffering does not reflect a basic condition of the world and, therefore, of human existence. It only reflects ignorance, stupidity, greed – all avoidable afflictions. Now the laws to be obeyed both by gods and by humans form a perfect abstract order. Again human life and reality are separated by an abyss: stupidity and disorder here, a perfect but inhuman order there.

Now let me make a few footnotes, partly repeating what I already said. My first footnote is about the role of the arts. Speaking from a modern point of view there are the arts, the sciences, there's philosophy, politics, religion and stuff like that. What can we say about the theatre? There are now lots of old plays. They are repeated again and again. Every young producer and every not-so-young actor dreams of putting his particular wrinkle on Lear, or Faust. Things were different in ancient Greece. A tragedy was performed once – and that was that. Later, in Alexandria, philologists started collecting editions – but not for performances. Eighteenth-century music was treated in a similar way. People like Haydn or Mozart conducted one of their symphonies once – and *basta*. The idea that you have a collection of masterpieces from the past which remain in the chest of cultural treasures and from there affect everything with their smell, started in the nineteenth century and it has not improved matters. Movies and rock music are much closer to the old idea of fresh invention than the established music and theatre business.

My second footnote is about intellectuals. I shall have to say a lot about these birds later on – for now let me just make a few remarks. Xenophanes and Plato were 'intellectuals' in the sense that they were dedicated to a kind of thinking that clashed with what happened around them. Well, in a way, the tragedians were also 'intellectuals'; however there was a great difference between them and the philosophers. The philosophers were read by a few people and they felt they were above their less sophisticated critics. The tragedians were seen by many and they felt they had to please their audience. They rewrote their unsuccessful plays and tried new and, they hoped, better versions of them. This did not turn them into fawning imitators of fashion. On the contrary; starting from what was common to all, they tried to lead their audience by means that were understood by all into new and as yet unchartered territory. This, you can believe me, is much harder than figuring something out by yourself and then offering it to a public that has been badgered into believing that it is up to them to understand the profundities of their 'intellectual leaders'.

Discussion

QUESTION: Do you believe in God?

FEYERABEND: I don't know. But I am certainly not an atheist or a conceited agnostic; it takes a whole life to find out about these matters. I have a feeling that some kind of supreme bastard is around there somewhere. I'm working on it.

QUESTION: What is your opinion about the idea of a natural, cosmological order which comes from a general idea of legal or social order?

FEYERABEND: You mean what is my opinion about the assumption that there is a link between scientific laws and the social order that discovers them? The assumption is quite plausible. Another question is what comes first, social laws or natural laws. To my mind this question doesn't even make sense. At any rate, today the two areas are definitely separated. Let me ask you a question. Do you assume that some people first fixed a certain social order, that next they started thinking about the universe and that they finally projected their social order on to the universe – is that the idea you have in mind?

QUESTION: Yes, but there is a well-known author, Rodolfo Mondolfo, who produced this idea. I believe that Jaeger proposed the same idea.

FEYERABEND: Well, you can find correlations but you can't find what comes first and what comes after. Let's go back to hunters and gatherers: they had to know a lot about the world to survive. And also about the seasons, because the fish go upstream at a certain time of the year – and so on. To know the seasons they had to have some knowledge about the movement of the sun. Scratchings were found on bones dating 30,000 years back and these scratchings correspond to the periodicity of the moon – apparently, days were counted by the moon while the seasons were counted by the sun. Did they get this idea from the social structure in which they lived? Well, hunters and gatherers had hardly any fixed social structures. Nevertheless, they had some ideas on astronomy and they had to have them in order to survive. So I think that saying that it was their social structure that made them astronomers means going the wrong way. Everybody, no matter what social structure they belong to, must know geography, astronomy and so on in order to survive. Mondolfo I do not know, Jaeger I have read but forgotten – but the question is not what this or that author has said – the question is what is plausible.

QUESTION: Just a short comment on modern theoretical physics. Perhaps I missed your point, but it seems to me that the idea that physical laws are invariant forces is not an *a priori* of modern theoretical physics. There would be thousands of physicists happy to see facts or events which are better explained assuming a violation of these invariant forces – time or space. So it is not something which is peculiar . . .

FEYERABEND: True, this idea that basic laws cannot contain any space–time parameters is not universally accepted, but it is a very popular idea! When there is a violation of a symmetry most physicists try to find a more general symmetry of which the broken one is a special case. Why was classical mechanics so popular? Because it seemed possible to explain all effects with its help. Why was it changed to special relativity? Because one was not content just to add special effects to it.

QUESTION: Yes, but this is an assumption because this is enough to explain facts. If you have facts not explained by this assumption, they are ready to change, they would be happy to change it. If you have facts, events, which demand that we should change the laws they don't ask for anything better – it is not an *a priori*.

FEYERABEND: You mean, they should change their laws into laws which are not time-invariant?

QUESTION: It does not matter. Any event which would introduce evolution in modern theoretical physics would be welcome.

Grazia Borrini-Feyerabend: Could I also intervene as a physicist, because for some time I've played that game. I would tell you that whatever I did was not open to that kind of stuff. What I would do was get some data and try to fit them into some laws that I knew were there. And maybe one day, I had eaten something bad at dinner and in the morning I would think that all the laws were rubbish, but it was never part of my daily work. I'm pretty sure that the idea to fit something in what is already there drives the great majority of scientists today.

FEYERABEND: There are laws which have a time-parameter or a space-parameter in them, or both, but hardly any scientist would regard them as basic laws. I admit this is a prejudice – why should we not all be involved in a grandiose process that is not the outcome of the workings of space–time-independent laws? It is a very old prejudice which, as I said, goes back to Parmenides' argument that Being is, not-Being is not and that change, which would be a transition from Being to not-Being, is non-existent. There were a few scientists who suggested putting in a time-parameter; if I remember correctly, Dirac was one of them. But their ideas never became very popular.

People do look forward to finding violations of basic laws because 'that is progress', not because they like laws with parameters in them, but because the violations may guide them to better and more general basic laws. Of course, in elementary particle physics you have high theory and you have phenomenology. Phenomenology is studied by guys who do curve fitting. They are satisfied with what they get at this level, just as experimental physicists are content with finding a nice way of producing some specific results. As a matter of fact, many experimentalists are suspicious about theory. They think that they, not the theoreticians, are in touch with reality. But then the high theoreticians try to find a general formula that can give them both the curves and the results. Very often the curve fitters abandon their 'raw data' and replace them with the data suggested by their curve. That can be rough on scientists who try a new approach and are criticized because their approach does not seem to fit 'the facts', which means the curve-fitted facts. Feynman tells an interesting example of this. Also there is a kind of ordering of scientists. This is very interesting for it again reflects some very old attitudes: on top are the theoreticians, then come the curve fitters and at bottom the fact finders. Not everybody accepts that ordering – but it is very popular. Theoreticians are better paid and more revered; non-scientists have pictures of Einstein or Bohr in their offices and even at home – hardly anyone uses Michelson as an icon. About a year ago a guy wrote me that he believes that theoreticians are even thought to have more sex appeal than experimenters who are dealing with rough matter. The same situation existed long ago – artisans did many useful things but philosophers denied that they had 'knowledge'.

QUESTION: You are talking about an order, in a way there is a tension towards an order, whereas he is talking about different laws that can be in conflict with each other. But in the end, the order still remains. They work out an order to make two different laws live together or these laws clash together and are destroyed and a new order comes out. The final point is: there is in politics, in social science, this tension towards finding out an order, and this order may well be basically compatible with the presence of laws which seem to be intrinsically clashing with each other. It is not necessary to have coherence in order to have an order in a way.

FEYERABEND: But that is what I just said – there are different groups and they are interested in different kinds of order. Some prefer a more 'elementary' kind of order, others a more abstract kind. Also more 'primitive' kinds of order are often preserved in the next step. In astronomy we had Ptolemy. He suggested a schema where each planet was calculated in a special and different way. Then there was Copernicus, who had one arrangement for all the planets. However, if one wanted to calculate, say the path of Mercury, one had still to make special assumptions that differed from those made in the case of, say, Mars. So there was a larger order which to a certain extent preserved the differences of the previous system. Then came Newton and with him a space–time independent law. Still, the old differences were preserved as differences of approximation. In the *Oresteia* we have the old law of the Furies, the new law of Apollo and in the end a 'synthesis' of the two.

QUESTION: When you have this order or this law, do you use it to predict, to describe or to explain?

FEYERABEND: Well, different people do different things. Some people say 'we're no metaphysicians, we don't explain, we just predict'. Some other people say 'we can explain what happened' and then they proceed and give what they call an explanation which in most cases is a little richer than a prediction. There are always different parties, but today most of them, in physics at least, like basic laws that are space–time independent.

2

The Disunity of Science

Last time I gave you a long quotation from Jacques Monod, the molecular biologist. He described what to him seemed to be some depressing features of modern science. 'By a single stroke', he wrote, the idea that objective knowledge – by which he meant knowledge not involving purposes – was the only source of truth 'claimed to sweep away the tradition of a hundred thousand years, which had become one with human nature itself. It wrote an end to the ancient animist covenant between man and nature, leaving nothing in place of that precious bond but an anxious quest in a frozen universe of solitude.'[1] Monod admits that the idea has not been generally accepted; that there are many people around for whom it is only part of the whole story, and perhaps not even a significant part. Still, it 'commands recognition' – and why? 'Because of its prodigious power of performance.'

At first sight the quotation sounds rather profound. But let us see what happens when we take a closer look. The objectivist point of view, Monod says, 'wrote an end to the ancient animist covenant between man and nature.' What does that mean? Does it mean that there once was a covenant and that materialistically inclined scientists dissolved it? That they had the power to dissolve the covenant? That the covenant was like a political agreement that could be changed by a one-sided decision, provided the decision was made by scientists? And that we, who have nothing to do with science, are left with the consequences? And how was the decision made? Did the scientists who accept the objectivist point of view meet at a conference and there vote to rescind the covenant? Was it that easy? Besides, there never was a meeting of this kind. Scientists have no loyalty to covenants; most of them lack the historical knowledge to even know about them, so why should they be asked to vote and, when asked, take the whole enterprise seriously? Or does the passage assert that an idea, not human beings, dissolved the covenant? This is an interesting assumption – but again, what does it mean? It is true that the rise of a science denying purposes occurred side by side with developments which loosened the connection (not any 'covenant') between humans and nature and which by now have disfigured large parts of the Earth. But it is not at all certain that science or its materialistic aspects caused these developments. Greed, lack of foresight, social tendencies unknown to the participants, the rise of capitalism did. Besides, Monod observes, and correctly so, that the 'frozen universe of solitude' did not win acceptance – it only 'commanded recognition'. Now what does that mean? Does it mean that lots of people are now studying the matter? That is certainly not true. Peruvian peasants never heard of the affair and I doubt that they soon will. And nobody knows what their reactions will be when (if) that happens. Does it mean that anyone, no matter of what gender, profession, religion, scale of income is obliged to pay attention to scientific objectivism? Using general notions, with no relation to people like you and me, it almost sounds as if Monod were stating such an obligation. That gives the whole passage a religious flavour except that religious leaders long ago have learned to speak in more personal terms ('Jesus died for you and me and everyone . . .'). At any rate, it is rather surprising to find religious gestures in an essay implying the end of all religion.

Next question: materialism – for that's what the world view described by Monod amounts to – 'commands recognition because of its prodigious power of performance.' Does this mean that we are supposed to pay attention to anything showing a 'prodigious power of performance' – no matter what the substance of the performance? That we must pay attention to materialism although its artistic 'power of performance' has been small, almost nil? Although it did not make people kinder, more loving and less selfish? Though it did not reduce the number of wars in the world or feed the hungry? These are important tasks – but what has materialism done about them? Very little, it seems. Of course, Monod did not think of music when writing his essay. What he meant when talking about 'power of performance' were certain arcane scientific results. But if that is all he can produce then the reply might well be that we are interested in other and more urgent matters.

So far I have moved outside Monod's circle of values. For Monod 'performance' means special scientific results and he takes it for granted that a field that produces such results – and nothing else – is very important indeed. And I asked why composers, prostitutes, painters, peasants, mothers should accept his standards of importance. Why they should even care about them. Is there any link between the results and the lives of outsiders? Scientists and their admirers assume, no, they take it for granted that there is such a link: the results are information about the world we inhabit – they tell us about 'reality'. Myths, art works, dreams, fairytales may sound as if they were speaking about a real world. Yet they are mere fantasies; they are epistemological fluff. Science alone, and this means its statements and the world views constructed from them tell us what really happens. So let us now take a look at this assumption. And to please scientists, let us examine it from within the circle of their standards and values. There is no obligation to enter the circle. But it is interesting to see what happens if we do.

The performance of science, says Monod, forces us to pay attention to the corresponding world view. What 'commands recognition' are not just particular techniques or special laws; what commands recognition is the house philosophy which scientists connect with them. For many scientists this house philosophy is materialism: the world is without purpose; it is a 'frozen universe of solitude'. This is what 'reality' looks like. Why should a depressing reality like this 'command recognition'? Because of 'its prodigious power of performance'; performance now being defined in terms of scientific results. Science is successful; all we can do is to shut up and pay attention to its ideology.

But is science successful? And do we have to shut up? And is there a single scientific world view?

At this point the temptation to be profound and to give a clever answer becomes very great indeed. New Age intellectuals especially try to show their sophistication by pointing out, with an air of superiority, that materialism has been refuted by science itself. Quantum mechanics, they say, implies that the major features of a materialistic world are not simply there, but appear when observers make an appropriate move. Otherwise it does not even make sense to assume their existence. Materialism, accordingly, does not describe the world as it is 'in and for itself'; it describes an aspect of an otherwise unknown entity. The aspect is not unimportant; entire sciences have been created to explore its properties and a large part of Western Civilization is involved in making it more specific and detailed. But it is not all there is and it does not exist independently of the actions of materialists.

This is a decisive argument indeed and I do not deny its force. But we can dethrone materialism with far less complicated weapons and using a much smaller army. All we have to do is to use our common sense. This, it seems to me, is a very important point. The errors of those for whom materialism has killed all alternatives are not sublime distortions of thought which respond only to equally sublime methods of investigation; they are gross mistakes and they can be corrected with the help of a few platitudes. In other words – you can criticize science without becoming a scientist yourself. More especially, you can criticize scientific demands – demands for more money, more power, greater influence in politics and especially in education – without becoming a scientist. A democratic criticism of science not only is not an absurdity – it belongs to the nature of knowledge. I do not say that such a criticism is easy and that you won't have to do much work. The jurors in a trial involving experts or the inhabitants of a country blessed with a nuclear reactor must study documents and listen to experts. However they can judge what they have heard or read without taking five semesters of physics I and II and three semesters of calculus and algebra and so on. Let me show you how, starting with the second of the three questions I asked above, namely, do we have to swallow 'the scientific world view'?

You all may have heard of arithmetical horses and counting dogs. They can still be seen in some circuses. The trainer brings them in and the audience gives them simple problems. For example, how much is four times three; or how much is twelve divided by six. The horse starts tapping out the answer: one, two, three, four and so on up to twelve in the first case – and there it stops. The dog barks – one, two, in the second case. They are always right – or almost always. But that does not matter. Even scientists make mistakes. How did the trainers get the idea that their animals might be able to do simple calculations? Why did they start training them? They assumed that animals have minds and that they are capable of reasoning. It was this assumption which guided their actions and, eventually, showed a 'prodigious power of performance'.

Well, we know now, or at least we think we know that the dogs and horses did not really count. They reacted to minute motions on part of their trainers. In the first case the horse started tapping out the answer – one, two, three . . . ; when it reached the twelve the trainer, unknown to himself, relaxed a little. That's what the horse was reacting to. When the trainer did not know the answer, the horse didn't know the answer either. Thus an idea which, because of its 'prodigious power of performance' 'commanded recognition' turned out to be mistaken. Was this an accident, or something to be expected?

To find out, let us compare the idea – animals can reason – with their performance. We see at once that the idea goes beyond merely describing the performance. It does describe the performance, yes, but it also asserts that the animals knew how to calculate. Now you may say that this was a very natural assumption to make. It was indeed – but even the most humble magician knows how to deceive people by putting them in situations in which the 'natural assumption' is the wrong assumption. So, we have to distinguish between a performance and the ideology that encourages the performance or seems to be supported by it. This ideology may continue to produce the expected results. On the other hand, it may run into obstacles. It is therefore possible, at any point in time, to accept the performance and to reject the ideology.

Molecular biology – the subject Monod was writing about – got far by renouncing purpose and trying to ensure the 'objectivity' of its results. It got far by adopting a materialistic research program. It had great ancestors. Astronomy, too, got far by denying the divinity of the sun, the moon and the planets. This makes materialism a possible world view; it does not force us to accept it. The reason is again that materialism is much more than a summary of its successes. It predicts that the materialistic research program will continue to be successful and it asserts that the successes are not some kind of trick but reveal the real nature of our world. Those who detest materialism either for personal reasons or because they belong to a sect with strong spiritualist leanings are therefore free to accept whatever useful things the materialistic ideology has produced without accepting materialism itself. They may not be acting in the 'natural' way magicians are counting on when producing their tricks; however, they are not acting illogically and besides, they have great scientists on their side. Thus it was quite 'unnatural', in the sixteenth century, to assume the motion of the Earth. Yet Copernicus, Kepler and Galileo made the assumption and started a new era of scientific research. At any rate, our choice of world views remains open no matter how many successes a particular world view can throw in our face.

This certainly is good news for religious maniacs who want to have their cake and eat it too. It is also good news for people who would like to approach nature in a more personal way but are being ridiculed for their 'superstitions'. It is good news for ecologists, agriculturists, conservationists of all sorts. Further, it is good news for those who believe that all cultures are in touch with reality, that we can learn from the most downtrodden and the most 'backward' people and that attempts to force 'genuine' knowledge on them shows not only disrespect but also a good deal of ignorance. Finally, and most surprisingly, the result is good news for scientists, for it turns out that it is a presupposition of scientific progress.

I already mentioned Copernicus and Galileo – but let me look at the matter in somewhat greater detail. It is often assumed that science starts from facts and eschews counterfactual theories. Nothing could be further from the truth. What is one of the basic assumptions of a scientific world view? That the variety of events that surrounds us is held together by a deeper unity. In the last lecture I told you that Thales was the first known thinker in the West to make such an assumption. Does the assumption agree with experience? Well, in a way it does and in a way it does not. Stones are very different from air. The difference could not be greater. But ice turns into water turns into mist. Does mist turn into air? Probably. Using processes and facts such as these as analogies we can postulate an underlying unity – but we do not experience, or observe this unity. We experience difference. So, if we take experience as our only guide we must say that there is diversity, not unity.

Now go on to Parmenides. One can regard Parmenides as a Thales going to the logical extreme. 'There is a unity, you say', Parmenides might have addressed Thales, 'a basic unity that underlies all diversity? Well, I don't see why you should stop at water. Being is much more basic than water; for water, air, fire and earth – they all are. That's what they have in common. But using Being as your basic substance you have to deny change. Why? Because Being is, not-Being is not, basic change would be from Being to not-Being. Not-Being is not, hence there is no basic change. You say that we perceive change? Well, the argument shows that we are mistaken – our common perception and the traditions based on it are all chimeras!'

Do not smile at this argument – its result has been accepted by almost all scientists. Basic laws, it is assumed, cannot contain any space–time parameters. There are a few physicists who are considering such laws – but their ideas are hardly popular. Classical physicists went even further. They distinguished between the objective world of scientific laws – and this world is without change – and the subjective world of our experiences. They ascribed reality to the former and regarded the latter as an illusion. Their theories supported them to a large extent. Classical point mechanics implies a minimum of change. All that happens is that certain configurations move reversibly from one moment to another which means that in a classical mechanical universe one moment is in no way different from any other moment. In a relativistic world even this minimum of change is laid out in advance. Here the world 'simply is; it does not happen. Only to the gaze of my consciousness, crawling upward along the lifetime of my body does a section of this world come to life as a fleeting image in space which continuously changes in time.' This is what Hermann Weyl, one of the outstanding scientists of his time, wrote in his book *Philosophy of Mathematics and Natural Science*.[2] Einstein went further. Addressing the sister of his departed friend Michele Besso, he wrote: 'For us who are convinced physicists the distinction between past, present and future has no other meaning than that of an illusion, though a tenacious one'[3] – which means that human lives and all the experiences assembled in their course, it means that birth, growth, death are 'illusions, though tenacious ones.' Popper was right when calling Einstein a four-dimensional Parmenides.

Now turn the argument around and assume that what happens in our lives counts as evidence to be used in our attempts to explore the world. Then the quotations just given inform us that this evidence, and as a matter of fact all pre-scientific evidence, conflicts with some very old and very basic scientific ideas. We have to conclude that science did not start from experience; it started by arguing against experience and it survived by regarding experience as a chimera.

Now take Galileo. Galileo, but also Descartes and later Leibniz, assumed that all processes in the universe obey inexorable laws. What was the evidence for this assumption? Experience informs us that some events obey laws while others show some regularity and many exceptions. The behaviour of the stars is lawful; the behaviour of clouds is not. The sun rises everyday but animals occasionally give birth to monsters. 'Natural is what occurs always or almost always,' said Aristotle, generalizing from this experience.[4] Aristotle also pointed out that strict laws are found in the heavens only; terrestrial events come and go in a much less regular way. To systematize these observations he assumed a two-tier universe with a 'super lunar' region containing all events above the moon and a 'sub lunar' region containing events on Earth and in the atmosphere. The idea that the whole universe, the heavens as well as the Earth obeys a single set of 'inexorable laws' (Galileo's expression)[5] clearly conflicted with the evidence I just mentioned and with its Aristotelian systematization. Were Galileo and Descartes saved by the openness of world views? And what have world views got to do with experience?

To answer the second question we have to distinguish between experience and empiricism. Experience is what we see, hear, smell and notice when entering as yet unknown regions. Empiricism is a philosophy or a world view which says that experience, when used properly, tells us exactly what the world consists of. Aristotle was an empiricist in the sense just explained. He assumed that experience mirrors the world provided the observer is in good condition (she is not drunk, asleep, besotted with love, etc.) and provided also there are no obstacles between the observer and her surroundings. Common sense is tied to this assumption and in turn lends support to it. But all of common sense cannot prove to us that experience does not conceal a complicated machinery which obeys inexorable laws and has only approximately regular effects, when its detailed workings are left out of account.

A third example is even more interesting because it is more technical and because some people believe that technicalities keep out error. After Newton had found his law of gravitation, he applied it to the moon and to the planets. It seemed that Jupiter and Saturn, when treated in this way, slowly moved away from each other – the planetary system seemed to fall apart. Ancient Babylonian records showed that the planetary system had been stable for a considerable time. Newton concluded that it was being kept stable by an additional force and he assumed that God from time to time intervened in the course of the planets. That agreed with his theological views. God, Newton believed, was not just an abstract principle. He was a person; he was concerned about his creatures and his interventions showed this concern. At any rate, there was a clash between the facts and Newton's law of gravitation used without additional assumptions. Did those who believed in 'inexorable laws' give up? They did not. Leibniz ridiculed Newton's god for being an incompetent universe-maker and declared that what god does once, he does in a perfect way – i.e. there are inexorable laws, they maintain the universe, and we have to find them: a religious argument kept the idea of a self-contained universe going.[6]

Now Euler, the Bernoullis and others replaced Newton's geometric methods by algebraic methods – an entirely new kind of mathematics was invented. Using this mathematics and pushing approximations further than anybody had done before, Laplace showed a century later, that the planetary system did not fall apart but oscillated with a very large period. 'I do not need this hypothesis', he said, when Napoleon asked him about the need for a divine being.

But that was not yet the end of the matter. It was discovered that the mathematical series Laplace had used, converged towards his results but diverged later on; a precise calculation would have given infinities. Then it was proven that the only way of making quantitative predictions was by means of series. But this meant that Newton's theory gave correct results only when used in an *ad hoc* way. It did not reveal a feature of the universe. Did scientists give up? No. The theory was plausible; it had astounding successes so it was retained despite the fact that, taken literally, it led to absurdities. Besides, many scientists were interested in predictions only and did not care about a metaphysical notion like 'reality'. Poincaré did care. Using a new type of mathematics, he recast the problem of stability – and now, it seems, we have at last a satisfactory solution.

Neither Thales, nor Parmenides, nor Galileo and not even Poincaré could expect success when contradicting experience and established opinions. On the other hand, there was nothing that could have stopped them from defending absurd ideas, meaning ideas that seemed 'unnatural' to their contemporaries. Of course, there was no guarantee that the defence would lead anywhere. But there was no proof of failure either. As it happened the absurd ideas produced results that gradually gained them acceptance, first among specialists, then among the 'educated public' and finally, with the rest.

Now look at the timescale. The ideas of Thales and Parmenides bore fruit only in the seventeenth century, with Newton's very successful but also very troubled views. Before that they were refuted by Aristotle, who reinstated common experience and common sense; they were again pushed back by the supporters of a strict second law of thermodynamics. Or take atomism. It arose as a speculative answer to Parmenides' denial of change. Why did Parmenides deny change? Because he admitted only one entity – Being. To preserve change the atomists postulated two entities, Being and non-Being, and they assumed that Being consisted of many pieces dispersed all over non-Being, or empty space, as we say today. They did not discover change and they did not refute Parmenides. Parmenides knew that change was the most obvious observable fact – but he denied that it was real.

The atomists wanted to bring science closer to common sense; they wanted to define reality in a way that did not deny the reality of the most obvious fact of our lives. They made what one might call a political decision; they decided to adapt their philosophy to life in the city – and they could do so, as we have seen. Atomism was refuted by Aristotle (take it from me, he really did refute it, using some very interesting arguments); it was rejected by most medieval philosophers. Taken up again by Galileo and Newton, it got into trouble in the nineteenth century when powerful facts in physics as well as in chemistry spoke against it. But then it produced successes in the kinetic theory (example: Maxwell's calculation of the variation of the viscosity of gases with temperature), was thrown out of electrodynamics and almost, of thermodynamics. It returned to the latter with Einstein's theory of Brownian motion and to the former with his photon theory and is now restricted again by complementarity, though not in molecular biology which sounds like a complicated version of good old Lucretius.

Now I want to take a short breath and summarize what I have said so far, in four propositions.

First proposition: The progress of science (in the sense of its defenders) depends on an openness of world views which conflicts with the totalitarian pronouncements of many of those defenders.

Second proposition: World views may take a long time, even centuries before they show results that 'command recognition'.

Third proposition: What 'commands recognition' in one community, is often without interest and even damaging in another.

Fourth proposition: A world view that contradicts 'well-established results' may clash with a fashion, or a temporary religious mania; however, it does not clash with the mania all scientists and science lovers embrace, namely, rationalism.

OK, you may say; introducing and defending world views that clash with established principles of modern science is not irrational and may even produce discoveries some time in the distant future. But there are problems that need to be addressed right now. It is therefore wise to stay with ideas which already have results instead of wandering off on a tangent. This is good advice, provided the results are relevant for the problems. Not all scientific results satisfy this condition.

First example: When President-elect Clinton started selecting his economic team many outstanding academic economists hoped, expected, took it for granted that they would be asked to be part of it. They were not asked. Clinton chose some relatively unknown people with no major academic achievements in economics, which means they had not written arcane papers, using advanced mathematics on profound theoretical difficulties. They had thought about practical problems instead. Moreover, they had thought about these problems in a manner that did not cut them off from the lives of ordinary people. Needs as experienced by local groups, expectations as expressed by the people on the spot and the suggestions they made, in non-technical and yet eminently realistic language seemed to them to be as important 'variables' as the abstractions of economic theory. Of course, these unmainstreamlike economists also used abstractions – everybody does – but their abstractions agreed with the abstractions of the local 'observers'. They were realistic in the sense that they had been tested and modified, and modified again by the experience of generations. It is true that academic economics is also tested; after all, academic economics still is an empirical science (though it hides its empirical content rather well). But the evidence here consists in the values of specially selected variables while the evidence of the locals is the large-scale experience of the world in which they live, with all its ramifications and idiosyncrasies. It is this experience of this world that needs to be maintained, or improved if one wants to help people, which means that it is this experience about this world that should be consulted, not the scientific evidence exclusively. The original sense of economics was 'the way of running a household'.

Aristotle understood the word in this way. I do not deny that modern economic theory can make a contribution to running a household, or a village, or a region, or even the entire world – though such a denial would not at all be unrealistic. What I do deny is that modern economic theory can replace the traditional ways without any loss of information or quality of life.

My second example is molecular biology – the subject in which Jacques Monod got his Nobel Prize. Like other research programs, molecular biology produced numerous results, some of general interest, others less so. Seduced by their success (which to them looked much bigger than it actually was), some molecular biologists thought that eventually all human problems might be solved and many new problems revealed by their methods. This was one of the motivations behind the 'human genome project' (another motivation was the money that is now flowing into the profession). When Daniel Koshland, the editor of the magazine *Science*, was asked if the millions poured into this type of research might not be better spent on helping the homeless he replied: 'What these people' – i.e. the people who asked the question – 'don't realize is that the homeless are disadvantaged'[7] – meaning that there was something wrong with their DNA and that the human genome project, when carried out, might be able to fix the matter. When? Certainly not now. Certainly not tomorrow. Today and tomorrow and for decades to come we better give our money to the human genome project. In the meantime hundreds or thousands of homeless may die. So, you see, the attempt to look for a better approach is not as unrealistic as it appears to those who claim to have 'results'. Relevant results are as enshrouded in the future as the results of less tried alternatives and, besides, there are approaches that work, here and now, though nobody has as yet christened them with the holy waters of the scientific faith.

Now forget about Clinton and Koshland and look at the matter from a more general point of view. One of the most conspicuous properties of laboratory science (where a laboratory may also be a mathematics workshop dealing with economic questions) is that it tries to eliminate 'disturbances'. Nature, scientists say, obeys basic principles – but she hides these principles behind all sorts of secondary processes. Nature must therefore be changed, the secondary events must be cleaned away, and the basic processes must be amplified until they can be perceived clearly and unambiguously. This is why scientists try to transform what they find and why they use the artificial results of the transformation and not undisturbed nature to infer general laws. The transforming agencies are powerful, invasive and they cost a lot of money – billions of dollars, in fact (just think of the Texas supercollider[8] and, again, of the human genome project). The process also works in reverse. What has been separated can be put together again – to a certain extent. Combining basic elements, science-based technologies have produced new gadgets such as the laser and the computer chip.

Note the attitude that underlies research of this kind. First, it is assumed that nature does not reveal her secrets willingly. She must be tortured, 'put on the rack' as Bacon put it. The basic laws are hidden behind false opinions and material obstacles which must be removed before objectivity and lawfulness are reached. Secondly, a scientist who knows the basic laws can judge a complex situation from afar, without inspecting it in person. Basic laws, after all, are valid everywhere. Neither they nor the specific conditions under which they work need an on-site observer to be identified. A few pointed questions to specially trained minions suffice. This attitude is rather widespread today. It is the reason why engineering schools increasingly move away from skills and towards an engineering science, why in some colleges molecular biology is replacing old-time medical instruction which was an instruction in skills, not just in pure knowledge and why evaluations; for jobs, stipends, scholarships, marriages and medical procedures are increasingly done by tests, not by a debate between the participants.

Now let us see where such an attitude leads and how successful one can expect it to be. Approaching a problem involving the interaction of humans and nature in a particular region, a problem of agriculture, for example, a scientist will first ask himself what the relevant variables are. They must be independent of the region and the feelings of those living in it. Only the values of the variables count. Why? Because otherwise an objective evaluation cannot be made. What is an objective evaluation? An evaluation based on those features of a situation one does not need to check in person. So you use variables you have introduced to be able to stay at home and you stay home because you are using these variables. This circularity occurs in many 'scientific' approaches. Next, we have a model. The model uses the best mathematics and the best empirical evidence available, where 'empirical evidence' is incoming information, sifted and streamlined in accordance with criteria that were developed in a laboratory, or in an office, not 'in the field' (with very few exceptions the mathematics, too, is office mathematics). We are miles away from the problem as it sits there in nature, with its plants, clouds, insects, humans, rodents, worms, etc. We are almost on another planet. Will the proposed solution help in the sense that it will improve the life of the locals? It may, in a laboratory-sense of 'improvement'. For example, it may raise the yearly production quota, the profit of the industries that are living off the land and, perhaps, the salaries of some of the locals. But 'life' is a matter of feelings, commitments and traditions. It involves generations and these must be given time to grow. It assumes a relative constancy of the habitat, not its destruction. Even an efficient industry needs a certain amount of 'nature' to survive. How can this kind of life be preserved and perhaps be improved a little? Is there any way of doing that?

Yes, there is. I already said that laboratory science and the industries that depend on it first eliminate 'disturbances' (to find the basic laws) and then recompose (to return to the complexity or the 'dirtiness' of real systems). The process of re-composition succeeds in simple cases. For example it succeeded with the planets, though the 'recomposition' here was purely theoretical. The process encounters difficulties when we move towards more complex systems such as a bridge, or a building. Successful architects and engineers therefore use theories combined with information that involves the way in which they, as experienced builders, react to the site. This information cannot be captured by an 'objective' report; the on-site experience is needed in addition to any description one might want to give, just as it is needed for judging or improving upon a work of art. Why is that so? Explicit thinking would take much too long to identify and to arrange all the elements which a thoroughgoing scientific analysis might discover. But experience can do the trick. After all, it also enables us to get along with still more complex systems, with humans, for example.

So let us now imagine a wood, or a field, with its delicately balanced ecology including the humans who have to live off the products of both. Is there a way of understanding such a system? Of finding out about its robustness and its limits? Of discovering what will be tolerated and what leads to irreversible change? Yes, there is. Whoever has lived in the region for generations has learned its peculiarities and its life rhythms and has stored this knowledge in eyes, ears, in the sense of smell, in feelings, in the mind, in the stories that are told to the community. In short, whoever has stored this knowledge not just in her/his mind but in her/his whole being, possesses information that is not contained in the results of a scientific appraisal. Only a little of this information can be written down or otherwise articulated – it shows itself in how things look and how they feel and it cannot be transferred to a person lacking the appropriate experience. However the knowledge is there – and it should be used. Again I do not suggest that science should be left out. Scientists discovered that practical knowledge can be mistaken in many ways (I am here mainly thinking of Pasteur's achievements). My point is that mistakes occur also on the other side and that practical knowledge can correct the shortcomings of an industrial-scientific approach. What we need therefore, is not an increasingly aggressive application of science that treats the locals as if they were idiots; what we need is a closer collaboration between experts and the people whose surroundings the experts want to judge, change, improve. Such an approach not only promises excellent results; it already achieved them in many countries. But results are not its only advantage. What is important is that the approach is much more humane than a purely objective procedure that treats ordinary people not as friends, or as potential collaborators, but as not always welcome because of rather disturbing sets of variables.

Let me now apply all the noise I have made so far to an event that still creates a lot of heat: the condemnation of Galileo. Was the Church entirely wrong, or was there some sense in its proceedings?

I start by explaining why a view may be false and yet show a 'prodigious power of performance'. Scientific theories and ideas in general are usually accepted because they have some advantages. They may put some order into material which at first sight looks unmanageable and chaotic. Linné's classification of animals and plants was of this kind. Astronomical theories have a similar function. The behaviour of the fixed stars, the sun, the moon and the planets is not easy to figure out. But once you know that the fixed stars rise and set in circles which are inclined towards the horizon; that the sun moves with them but also has a motion of its own on its own circle and contrary to the rising-and-setting motion, you will understand a little what is going on. You will not only understand, you will also be able to make some simple predictions. The motion of the planets remain. To master them, the ancient Greek astronomers invented a rather ingenious two-circle system. The first circle, the so-called deferent, goes around the Earth. The second circle, the epicycle, goes around a point that moves along the circumference of the deferent. The system can be modified in many ways. The Earth can be moved away from the centre and the centre of the epicycle can be made to rotate around another eccentrically situated point, further circles can be added – and so on. Given the correct constants the system made excellent predictions in some areas, not so good predictions in others. In this it was not at all different from even the most advanced scientific theories.

Next assume that the system is embedded in a world view where space is centrally symmetrical, dynamically active and where the Earth is at rest in the centre. Such a world view makes lots of sense. The Earth is indeed seen to lie in the centre of all planetary circles (which now include the sun and the moon) and the unhindered motion of terrestrial objects seems to be determined by space, not by the Earth: fire moves away from the centre but the Earth, which is also at the centre, could not possibly have anything to do with its motion.

Now add Aristotle's two-tier universe: perfect circles in the heavens, up and down motion on the Earth. This universe can be interpreted in a strict way and in a more lenient way. In the first case all planets move in circles around the centre. Why in circles? Circles alone guarantee the lasting lawfulness that seems to be the heavens' property. You will notice at once that the epicyclical system does not agree with this world view. Here the planets do not move around the centre; they move around a mathematical point which moves around the centre. For 'mathematicians' in the sense in which this word was understood in the later Middle Ages this was no problem. What they had done was to provide a model for calculation. Neither they nor their modern successors assume that models are direct pictures of reality.

Now, make a further addition. Add Christianity. What do Christians believe? That God sent his only son to the Earth to save humanity. Through the firm and regular heavens Christ descended to the valley of tears, the Earth, to save humanity and especially the poor and disadvantaged. This story gives powerful meaning to the geocentric two-tier universe. Christ was not a space traveller who got crucified now in the one, now in the other galaxy. He came to a singular point, the place where humanity lived, a place at the bottom of the universe and made it even more singular by his suffering. Poems, frescoes, churches of immense dimensions, altar pictures, music, all the arts and all the sciences were inspired by this event and gave testimony to the power of the faith.

Now come Copernicus and Galileo and they say that the sun is at the centre and that the Earth moves. This, they say, is the truth; the older views are mistaken. And, they say, there exist powerful arguments which show why it is the truth. What is a contemporary to do?

That depends on what his interests are. Leonardo Olschki[9] tells of a popular play of the early seventeenth century where the Earth is set in motion. Some people who liked to see plays did not seem to be upset. What a fantastic notion – a moving Earth! Well, you could almost see it, moving by the stars during the day and, more slowly, during the year. A dizzying experience indeed!

What about Christianity? That depends on the interpretation given to its basic myth and that in turn depends on the interpretation of the Bible. St Augustine read biblical events allegorically, as symbols of a deeper lying meaning. Such an interpretation is only loosely connected with 'the structure of the real world'. A change from geocentricism to heliocentricism need not affect it in any way. For the orthodox Catholic Church many biblical passages, passages concerning the shape of the universe included were literally true, provided there were no powerful secular arguments to the contrary. The idea of a flat Earth had been given up by the eleventh century; here the church had accepted the relevant scientific arguments. The idea of a central static Earth was still retained.

Like many far reaching decisions, both in the sciences and elsewhere, this was done partly on political grounds. Power (over minds and institutions) played as important a role then, in science as well as in religion, as it plays today. The decision had a component which many people, me included, are still willing to support. It is that the sciences are not the last authority on the use of their products, their interpretation included. Questions of reality are too important to be left to scientists (just remember Aristotle's reaction to Parmenides). Today the final decisions I am talking about are in the hands of political bodies; they are in the hands of a senate, or a local government, or of the National Science Foundation (which is a political, not a purely scientific, body) or a citizens' initiative. In the seventeenth century the Church played a large, though not an exclusive role.

There was also the world view of the common people. I say 'the world view of the common people' as if 'the common people' had been a continuous mass immersed in a coherent single world view. Such an idea can no longer be taken seriously. As Ginsburg and others have shown, different regions had vastly differing beliefs and practices with Christianity forming a vague and rather ambiguous background.[10] These scholars could even identify individuals who had developed particular and rather interesting though thoroughly idiosyncratic world views. At any rate, some communities were held together by strong common views. Was heliocentricism strong enough to remove these views?

This is the wrong way of putting the question. Ideas are not agents that do things. People are. So let us ask again: Were there any reasons for people strongly tied to a literal geocentric version of Christianity to drop this version and to adopt Copernicus instead? The question is still too 'objective'. It assumes 'reasons', i.e. things people ought to accept. So, let us ask again: Can we imagine that hearing of Copernicus such people will stick to their views? Yes, we can. Can we imagine that they will use reasons of their own? Yes, we can. What might some of these reasons be? A strong belief in the literal truth of the importance and the shape of Christ's journey. Is such a belief 'irrational' when compared with the 'scientific' arguments? It is 'irrational' when compared with the 'normal' reactions of the progressive party which however is as precarious as the normal reaction of the audience of a magician. It is not irrational when the nature of world views is taken into account. This nature permits any group to stick to any of its beliefs when it wants to and is not prevented by the general political situation.

Let me return to the attitude of the Church and again ask the question which our science freaks usually put at the head of all proceedings, namely: Was the decision of the Church a 'rational' decision?

That depends on what criteria of rationality you are going to choose. Modern scientists, experimentalists especially, are very strict. I doubt if Michelson would have given credence to an instrument as little understood as the telescope and I wonder what modern astronomers would have said when comparing the planetary predictions coming out of the Ptolemaic system with those of the early Copernicans. Sixteenth-century astronomers were familiar with the 'instrumentalist' interpretation of scientific theories, with the interpretation which recognizes that false views can do a good predictive job. Many of them accepted Copernicus – as a model, not as a true description of the universe. Here the church simply followed scientific precedent. Strict empiricists could not have been happy with Copernicus' assumption that earthy matter follows the travelling Earth wherever it goes – what was the evidence for such a strange and convenient force? (Why convenient? It helped Copernicus to overcome the difficulties of the dynamical arguments against the motion of the Earth.) Of course, the Copernican world view profited from the openness of world views I have explained above. It was a possible world view and could not be removed by intra-scientific arguments. But so was geocentricism which, moreover, had the advantage of familiarity and, for those reading the Bible in a literal fashion, the advantage of not destroying important meanings. These advantages count for little today when change, innovation, progress are not only intellectual manias but are sorely needed to keep the capitalist production machine going. But that only shows how little objectivity there is in objective scientific arguments.

So – what about Galileo? Was he a hero? A nut? A criminal? Like every human being he was a little bit of all these things and like every Italian he showed these character traits enlarged. Does 'humanity' owe him anything? 'Humanity' doesn't, only a few people do. Has he not improved 'our' view of the universe? Well, it depends whom you mean by

The Disunity of Science

'our'. Artists? I have no idea. Would a single Mozart symphony be different if Galileo had never lived? Nobody can say. Haydn's chaos music (of the creation) was allegedly inspired by having looked through Herschel's telescope. Well, Haydn did visit Herschel and he conversed at length with this fellow musician but Copernican arguments nowhere entered the scene. Galileo was part of a tradition that is very powerful today and which he improved in many ways – that is all we can say. The rest depends on what we think about this tradition. I have given you a few opinions on some of its aspects.

Let me add a footnote. You may have noticed that I don't proceed in a very systematic fashion. Well, we are living in a chaotic world and introducing a system into it means introducing an illusion. The footnote is this: In the next lectures I'll tell the history of certain ideas, starting from the ancient Greeks. The stories I shall tell you may be of some interest to you, just as stories. However, perhaps you will also learn something from these stories (if that's where your interests lie). You may learn that any idea that exists has faults and that even the silliest idea contains good points – for some people. Ideas are results of historical accidents, social forces and the intelligence of some individuals and the idiocy of others. One of the ideas that is floating around and which I would like you to approach in a more relaxed fashion is the idea that science tells you everything there is to be known about the world and that ideas which conflict with science are not worth considering.

I am amazed to see how widespread this view really is. For the past ten years I had a job in Switzerland, at the *Zürich Polytechnic*, one semester per year (the rest of the year I spent in California).[11] During my semester in Switzerland, a friend of mine and I ran a public seminar, once a week, from five to seven, in room F1 of the central building. Our audience was from one hundred to one thousand people, depending on the topic and the speakers; usually there were about 250 to 300 people. To start proceedings we invited three or four big shots; they gave talks, debated with

54

each other, then answered questions and objections from the public. On one occasion we invited four theologians: a Catholic theologian, a Protestant, a Moslem, and a Rabbi. We asked them to talk about the effect the rise of science has had on their religions. Was the situation now better than before Galileo, was it worse and, if the latter, in what respect. The Protestant and the Catholic theologians were very cautious. They did not dare to say a word against the sciences. When I challenged them their reply was: 'We have been burnt once, we don't want to be burnt again.' Discussing Galileo's case, the Rabbi and the Muslim were the much more straightforward. They said 'we love knowledge in any form,' thus recognizing that there are other forms of knowledge besides scientific knowledge.

Even the Pope, who can be quite aggressive when asked about the rights of women or the merits of liberation theology, is apologetic, subservient and downright cowardly in scientific matters.[12] Science, it seems, is an irresistible force. And this it is indeed but only if you believe in the promises and give in to the PR of the science-mafia. It is irresistible if you permit it to be so.

You may decide to take science as your guide not only in practical matters but also in matters of meaning, ideology or content of life. But you may also decide to take science as your guide in practical matters – and here science has been successful, but only to a certain extent – and build up the rest of your world view from entirely different sources.

Moreover, the people who say that it is science that determines the nature of reality assume that the sciences speak with a single voice. They think that there is this monster, SCIENCE, and when it speaks it utters and repeats and repeats and repeats again a single coherent message. Nothing could be further from the truth. Different sciences have vastly different ideologies. There is molecular biology and I told you what one of its practitioners believes. But there is also the theory of elasticity. Which world view does the theory of elasticity suggest? This is difficult to figure out. For some people elasticity is a peripheral subject which, naturally, is a special case of elementary particle physics, only nobody has yet shown that and nobody (among the people I am talking about) really cares. Others say that elasticity is a separate subject which has as little to do with elementary particle physics as it has to do with the Bible. There are scientists who eschew speculation and regard it as a piece of metaphysics. Many scientists of that creed avoided the general theory of relativity. Then there are speculators who don't give a damn about the details of the evidence. Radical empiricists are found in biology – but also in cosmology; Ambarzumyan is one of them; Halton Arp is another.[13] Molecular biologists are objectivist in a simple sense. For them, the basic entities are out there in the world, whether you look at them or not. But this is not the idea that comes out of quantum mechanics. Here your findings depend on your procedures – and so on.

So you see – the sciences are full of conflict. The one monster SCIENCE that speaks with a single voice is a paste job constructed by propagandists, reductionists and educators.

So far I have been talking about the physical sciences. But there is sociology, psychology and they are full of schools and dissension. Therefore, it is not only wrong to say 'we are forced to take science as our guide in matters of reality' – the advice simply does not make sense.

Discussion

QUESTION: Would you say that nowadays the prevailing conception among the scientists is that they are actually dealing with reality, as you were suggesting at the beginning? This might be the view that the layman has. I don't think it is the view of the scientists.

FEYERABEND: Well, as I said, there are many different kinds of scientists. There are scientists who deal with a basic theory which is supposed to apply to everything, and there are scientists who deal with restricted laws: For example, what happens to elementary particles under certain very restricted conditions.

And there are further scientists who do just curve fitting. They have a few results and they try to find the best curve between them. If you ask them if they think they are dealing with reality, some will say 'leave me alone, I've got nothing to do with that! I've got some nice numbers here and I am trying to connect them.' Other scientists may answer that they don't quite know. So there are different opinions.

Some of the scientists who invented the quantum theory were forced into questions of reality because of the paradoxes they ran into. In a way the paradoxes were similar to the paradoxes of a naive realism which says that what we perceive is also there. Push one of your eyes out of its normal position and the world looks double. Has it really doubled? Certainly not. Therefore we must become a little more careful. How? Well, that needs some thought. In the same way the paradoxes of quantum mechanics needed some thought devoted to the idea of what is real and what is not.

So, scientists have different official opinions on the matter of 'reality'. Apart from that they have their own private philosophies which they occasionally hide from their colleagues for fear of being ridiculed.

There's a large school in the sciences saying that if you come to basic laws, you cannot speak anymore of an observer-independent reality. In common sense and in the large scale, scientific reality is something that exists independently of whatever humans are doing. Humans are like aliens coming into a world which was there long before they even existed; they examine this world without disturbing it and find out its properties. Today many scientists say that this conception does not agree with certain very basic laws. Where did it come from?

One source may have been *Genesis*. According to *Genesis*, God created first the Heavens and the Earth, then a lot of other things and finally, human beings. God blew life into human beings, which made them strangers because now they had an element that was lacking in the created world.

Do the actions of human beings have an effect on the world? They certainly do. Think of the ozone hole. The United States, the whole of the American continent has been changed since it was invaded by the Europeans. It has changed quite a lot since that time: rivers now have different beds, the climate has changed and also the quality of the water, entire species have disappeared, instead we have blocks of concrete everywhere and so on.

Now, the realists say that what we see and the regularities we find are not reality, because reality is deeper than what we see. Do you remember what I told you about Parmenides? He said that there is a reality which never changes and that our lives which are built on change are an illusion. So the fact that there are lots of changes going on as a result of the presence of human beings indicates, to those who believe in unchangeable objective facts and laws, that these unchangeable objective facts and laws must be very different from what we directly perceive, and this means they must be very different from the real life of normal human beings.

Materialists, on the other hand, assume that the observer is part of the world, that the interactions between the observer and his surroundings are part of the world and that both obey unchanging fundamental laws. So it is not anymore so easy to separate humans from the rest of the world. Where will you put the cut between the two? If you assume that there is an immortal soul and a special perceptual ability, that's one thing. But if you assume it's the same inside and out, where will you put the boundary?

QUESTION: My question may seem obvious and it may be that you have already answered it. There is a vast debate in the social sciences on whether one can just describe and understand reality (social reality) or else can even explain reality. I wonder if the debate is present in other sciences and if there is a clear position on this.

FEYERABEND: There has been a long debate in the philosophy of science and in the physical sciences about explanation, description and prediction. Does a scientist explain or does he just describe or predict? As far as I can see the problem has not been solved. I would say that explaining means referring things you have noticed to things you think are real and really connected with the case before you. Otherwise you merely describe. Does this mean you 'explain' the unknown by what is already known? No, it does not, for the real entity you are referring to may have been introduced together with the explanation and may not have been known before. And this seems to be the normal case. For example, when people introduced things like atoms to explain winds, heating and so on, they introduced a new entity to explain phenomena that were well known. So, you actually explain the known by the unknown and not the unknown by the known, as many people assume. And I would also say that unless there is a difference in practice between explanation and mere description, unless those who think that they explain act somewhat differently in their research from those who say they merely describe, it is just a quarrel about words.

Let me give you an example taken from the physical sciences. A stone falls to the ground. Somebody wants to know why. Somebody else introduces the force of gravitation which the Earth exerts on the stone. Is this an explanation? Yes, you may say, for we have now not only the stone falling, we have also something else, the force the Earth exerts on it. We have a real connection between the stone and the force and with it the desired explanation.

So far so good. Now listen to Bishop Berkeley. Reacting to the explanation (and to Newton's theory of gravitation in general) he asked: 'What do you mean when you speak of the force of gravitation? What is the cash value of that statement? Its cash value is that stones fall down; planets go round the sun and so on. So, gravitation is a summary of many events, among them the stone falling down; it is not a new entity.' Now, if you interpret gravitation as a summary of many events, then deriving the falling stone from the law of gravitation is not an explanation: you are just using one element of the summary.

So it all depends on what you think about the terms by means of which we explain. If you think they designate real processes then you can say 'we made a discovery, therefore we explain.' If you regard them as summaries, then you merely describe. At any rate, the term 'explanation' has many meanings and that is one of them, namely the meaning that was given to it in the philosophy of science of about forty years ago.

QUESTION: I would wish to defend a little bit philosophy and especially Plato's philosophy against Paul's attack. Yesterday you said that tragedy in ancient Greece was essentially a beautiful synthesis between different forms of life and that since Plato this kind of synthesis was split. And of course you quote Plato's attack in his *Republic* against tragedy and so on. But after Plato there was also Aristotle, the first real theoretician on tragedy. But even Plato's attitude towards tragedy is very ambiguous and complex. I'm reading the *Symposium* these days, and in the end, when all the guests have fallen asleep totally drunk, only three people remain clear-headed: Socrates, Agathon the tragedian and Aristophanes the comedy writer. And then Socrates tries to show them that a real writer, a true author, should be able to write both comedies and tragedies. I think that this is a key to understand the *Symposium* and through it Plato's philosophy itself, that is, his conception of philosophy as a tragicomic enterprise.

Yesterday you stressed the happy end in the *Oresteia*; on the other hand, Sophoclean tragedy is very gloomy. Maybe the split that you denounce in philosophy was accomplished in tragedy. And maybe, since Plato, philosophy has been trying to rebel against this split, because tragedy wasn't anymore able to unify in a synthesis the different aspects of life.

Maybe the real utopia of philosophy was to reconstruct the unity of the different forms of life – good, beautiful and truth – together. Maybe what philosophy has been trying to do after the failure of tragedy is to continue this attempt at unifying the world and human life.

FEYERABEND: It is true that yesterday I said that Plato had a rather negative attitude towards tragedy but, I added, 'in Book X of the *Republic*'. Not generally. Plato is not all in one book. He changes constantly, and it is interesting to see the context in which he makes his criticism of tragedy.

In the eighth book he mentions arithmetic, geometry, music and astronomy. These subjects all have a practical side and except astronomy, also a theoretical side, which means a side dealing with reality. He hopes that future research will find this theoretical side in astronomy too. Now, in Book X he talks about another group of subjects which, according to him, are completely useless – in this particular book, not elsewhere in his dialogues – because they cannot be supplemented by a theoretical part and they deceive. At the end of his criticism he says something very interesting: 'However, as we ourselves have been so much moved by the tragic muse (some say that Plato wrote a tragedy when he was young and then destroyed it) we urge those who favour her to defend her, either in prose or in verse, and in this way to show her merits.' What he is saying is that the last word has not yet been spoken. A defence was indeed made by Aristotle.

Tragedy itself was not just one thing, it was many. I mentioned Aeschylus, who is democratic-rationalistic in a vague sense. I also mentioned Sophocles, who is entirely different. In Aischylos human beings with the help of the gods can work their way out of trouble. In Sophocles this is impossible because the world is inherently contradictory; it has what one might call a tragic dimension.

In the *Eutyphron*, which is an early dialogue, Plato criticizes this view by asking the question: 'Are good and bad decided by the gods? Or do the gods decide what is good and what is bad by looking at the idea of the good?' And Plato says that the gods look at the idea of the good and therefore the tragic contradiction cannot occur. By implication he criticizes, I think, Sophocles for giving the impression that tragic conflicts are inherent in the nature of things and cannot possibly be removed. So Plato wants tragedy to be replaced by a view of good and bad which permits an escape from the bad and which doesn't have this tragic conflict in it. And, at least in this dialogue, this is what philosophy is supposed to do. Whom shall we follow – Sophocles or Plato?

I would say that it's up to whoever considers the question. On the one side we have the old tragedy which contains both possibilities. On the other side we have a reduced, less complex view of life, offered not to the large audience of the tragedies but to a small elite of philosophers.

Now philosophy had little effect on the citizens of Athens; what had an effect was Socrates standing at corners bothering everybody – that was a philosopher for them. People knew that Plato existed, but his ideas were not so well known except by a small elite. Therefore the solution, if there is one, is a solution for elites only, the general populace is left by the wayside.

Was there an improvement? Tragedy presented a richer view of life than philosophy, as supported by Plato. This richer view was accessible to more people, to the whole population, in fact, and they could understand it. Philosophy? Dried up and elitist by comparison, even the philosophy of Divine Plato.

Let me finish with an anecdote reported by Aristotle. Plato spent most of his time at his academy but once he gave a public lecture on The Good. Lots of Athenians came because they thought he would teach them how to improve their marriage, how to run a better household – and so on. Instead Plato talked about the unit, the division of the unit, the incommensurability of the division with the unit and so on. After five minutes there was nobody left except his pupils. Plato was not a popular philosopher. And, you see, this would not have happened in tragedy.

QUESTION: Dante's Comedy is both a tragedy and a comedy . . .

FEYERABEND: It depends whose definitions of tragedy and comedy you are going to use; there are many definitions. Plato would have called it a tragedy, for he called also the Homeric poems a 'tragedy'. According to Aristotle, Corneille or Lessing a tragedy must have a simple plot and it must contain conflict. Dante's plot is complex, 'episodic', as Aristotle would say, and without conflict. Hence, according to Aristotle, Corneille or Lessing the Comedy would be an epic, not a tragedy.

QUESTION: But Dante is full of friction . . .

FEYERABEND: It has friction but no tragic conflict.

3

The Abundance of Nature

Well, I have been talking about some ancient Greeks and I have been talking about some modern scientists and about the problems which both had to face. I also talked a little about the relation between artisans, farmers, engineers, healers, bird watchers who were practical people and 'scientists' meaning by the latter people who rely on abstract principles, not on practical experience. As a matter of fact this characterization of scientists is a little unfair; it is true of theoreticians but does not apply at all to experimentalists. Philosophers of science, to mention this disreputable profession, have been in the habit of regarding theory as the centre of science. For the logical positivists, for example, science was a system of statements and theories that tried to bring these statements into some kind of order – they were statements of a special kind. Can you imagine that? There are these philosophers, and they are intelligent people and all they see when looking at science is *statements*. They do not see laboratories; they do not see the fights scientists and politicians engage in to settle financial questions; they do not see the large telescopes, the observatories, the staff buildings, the staff conferences, the effects of an asshole in power on his underlings – they see only statements. Well, naturally there are statements in the business, there are numbers, papers, computer printouts and although they are not always legible, one can define 'statement' widely enough to say that they all contain statements. But the experimental level – well, for these philosophers it is as relevant to science, so it seems, as a typewriter is to a poet. It is a means of producing statements.

Let's not be too unjust to these philosophers. They are part of a long tradition. I'll soon tell you a little more about this tradition, when it started (always restricting myself to the West, which means Greece in our case), how it works today. The tradition has many practical side effects. Theoreticians are thought to be more intelligent, they are paid better and they have a greater reputation than experimentalists. They are supposed to be the people who decide about reality and other such arcane matters. Now it is true that facts by themselves don't tell you anything. Assume that all you know is that the stars rise and set. What do you know? Very little. They may rise because that's how they move. They may rise because the Earth rotates. They may rise and set because everybody is a little dizzy. Everybody? Just remember the moon. It looks large when it rises, much smaller when it culminates. Same about the constellations. Jumping up from the horizon Leo looks enormous – crossing the meridian it has become a pussycat. Everybody sees things that way and following experience Aristotle conjectured that the terrestrial atmosphere acts like a lens and magnifies celestial bodies and arrangements when they are on the horizon. Today the received theory is that it is all an optical illusion. So, *facts* by themselves don't tell us anything. It needs *thought* to find out what they mean. So far so good. But to assume further that only theoreticians think and that experimentalists do not – that is going too far. After all, what experimentalists offer are not *facts*, but *effects* of a recondite nature which reveal the workings of basic laws in a rather direct way. The theoreticians can give them some guidance but moving in the upper spheres of thought they have no idea of all the disturbances, all the 'dirt' that is interposed between high theory and the ordinary circumstances from which they are supposed to start. So, first on their list are efforts to remove the dirt. And here it does not suffice to offer a more or less 'clean' effect – the absence of disturbances must be shown in a convincing way. After all, every theory has opponents. And every alleged proof of a theory will be examined very, very carefully by these opponents. A good experimenter makes this examination so difficult that most people are not willing to even start, which means that a good experimenter must be kind of a rhetorician. His experiments must be powerful rhetoric. Michelson's experiment – the second version – was excellent in this respect, so excellent in fact, that it is now regarded as a direct demonstration of a basic principle of modern physics. So it is not just the theoretician who thinks; the experimenter thinks as well and in a way that differs from the thought of the theoretician. The theoretician's rhetoric is verbal, or mathematical. The experimentalist's rhetoric appeals to the aesthetic sense – it is visual and practical.

There are many other properties that distinguish the experimenter from the theoretician and that make the level of experiment a self-contained culture within science. More recent philosophers of science and historians especially are recognizing this. There is a nice book by Ian Hacking, *Representing and Intervening* in Cambridge University Press, that shows the special ways in which instruments are used, treated, improved and their results connected with theory.[1] Nancy Cartwright has gone further. She wrote a book *How the Laws of Physics Lie* (Oxford) where she argues that most high theory is false if experimental results are taken as a measure.[2] Experimental results, experimental effects (which are more robust than results) and low-level laws which directly generalize from them, she says, are OK. So is phenomenology – in the sense in which this word is being used in high-energy physics. But high theory, though impressive, and connected to facts by many tricky arguments, does not report what happens, but provides a metaphysical framework which, when taken literally, must be regarded as false. So experimentalists and their pronouncements have had a kind of comeback in history and philosophy and also in areas where theoreticians and experimentalists work closely together and the old theory-bound philosophy is gradually being abandoned – by *reasonable* people. But there are still lots of people around who believe that it is theory which informs us about what holds the world together. Where does this idea come from?

I think it is an offspring of a very ancient belief. Most societies have practical rules and practical knowledge on which these rules are based. The practical knowledge is detailed and far exceeds what modern people, scientists included, have to offer in this respect. But many societies have also stories of a more general kind, stories which are not directly connected with their day-to-day experience but which provide a framework of meaning and explanation. Occasionally the general stories, or myths as they have been called, are in the hands of a special class of people with special authority. These people may be familiar with the practical knowledge possessed by the rest – but they know more! This assumption may be expressed by saying that they alone know while the rest just lives as their instincts and their memories tell them. Knowledge lies in the myth; it does not lie in the habits that guarantee survival. It does not matter that those relying on the myth occasionally give bad advice. For example, it did not matter that the myth-guided physicians in ancient Babylonia occasionally killed their patients while the practical healers were a little more successful. They knew more – this alone sufficed.

Now jump from here to Plato, to Book VII of his *Republic*, to be more precise. In this book Plato enumerates the practical branches which are useful for a society. He mentions four: arithmetic, geometry, music and astronomy. Arithmetic helps a general to count his troops and to distribute them in an adequate manner. Geometry is used in building, astronomy in navigation and for orientation in general. Music sets the mood which is important in war and peace. So all these subjects are *useful* to society. However, they do not on that account contain knowledge. A general may know how to count – that does not mean he knows what numbers are. A geometer may know how to design a building and dig a tunnel – but he does not know the nature of lines, areas, solids. And so on. Fortunately there exist subjects, parallel to the practical subjects that contain the relevant knowledge. Counting is explained by the principles of number theory which started with the Pythagoreans and gradually extended afterwards. Behind the practical knowledge of the architect lie the abstract principles – not the practical rules! – of the science of geometry. And music has the theory of harmony as a support. Only astronomy is as yet lacking a theoretical foundation, says Plato. How shall we obtain it? Not by *observing* the heavens which will give us an aching neck, but no knowledge. We obtain the needed knowledge by engaging in theory – by considering mathematical models, as we would say today. And indeed – the science of astronomy started from and progressed with the help of increasingly complex models which not only ordered 'the facts' but also decided what the facts were. Just remember the story of the great inequality of Jupiter and Saturn which I briefly sketched in the last lecture.

So a very modern idea which is taken for granted by many scientists and philosophers has very old origins. Actually, it has a double origin. It has an *intellectual origin* in the groups that started Western rationalism and a *'primitive'* origin in the myths that preceded it. What's the use of knowing that? Well, I think its use is very great. Those science-bound intellectuals who praise theory and look with contempt at anything that is not stamped head and bottom with scientific credentials can be reminded that they are themselves the unwitting defenders of ancient – well, let us say 'prejudices', for that's the word they are using to condemn whatever does not please them. That may give them pause, make them more critical, or more tolerant – at any rate they may look at their 'knowledge' in a new way. We are also invited to think a little more about the nature of scientific success.

Science, we are told, is very successful. And, so the tale continues, its success is due to observation and experiment. Well, in the last lecture, I gave you examples that throw serious doubt on this assumption. Important scientific principles were introduced *against* experience (or, later, experiment), not in conformity with it. One of the most basic principles is that there are laws which are valid independently of space, time, temperature and which hold during the first fractions of a second of our universe as well as today. Now if that is not a big myth, then I really don't know what is! But is it not true that the laws were confirmed and continue to be confirmed? I am not quite sure that is the case.

Galileo, Descartes and others believed in laws underlying all there is. In the nineteenth century this belief had led – not to a single basic science with many branches in different directions, but to a plethora of methods, assumptions, results. There exists a very interesting and most informative account of nineteenth-century science and philosophy by Theodore Merz – it shows how the situation really was.[3] There was the general belief that somehow this plurality was part of a comprehensive but as yet missing super-science. Some scientists even thought they already had this super-science – mechanics. However the detailed argument how, say, forgetfulness, or the process of meiosis can be obtained from mechanics was missing then and is missing now. Today quantum theory has replaced mechanics – still, the problem is as big as ever. Forgetfulness and meiosis are being treated in special sciences, and they are being treated very well – but the overall account, the detailed overall account, not just the *promise* is missing. Thus the relation between the belief in 'inexorable basic laws', the inexorable laws themselves, the sciences that contain them, the sciences that have principles of their own, not immediately relatable to the basic laws, and finally, experience or experiment is rather puzzling, to say the least. Can't we find out anything? We can find out a little by going back to the times when such overall principles were first discussed by intellectuals, i.e. by going back to Xenophanes, Parmenides and their immediate predecessors.

I told you that Xenophanes replaced the Homeric gods by a god-monster that was all thought, all vision, all power but without any vice. How did he get such an idea? Today there is a very simple answer to that question: Xenophanes was 'creative'. Well, this is an answer, but it does not explain anything. It says that he produced the idea all on his own. But we know that already! We know (or think we know – remember what I said about the ancient evidence!) that there was nobody else who had such ideas. Is there a better answer? Well, Karl Reinhardt in his book on Parmenides suggests that Xenophanes, or someone in his surroundings may have argued as follows:[4]

> God is one, or god is many.
> If he is many then they are either of equal strength, like the citizens of a democracy, or some are stronger than others.
> But gods are not like the citizens of a democracy.
> Nor, if they are stronger and weaker are the weaker ones gods, hence
> God is One.

A nice argument which, incidentally, shows the use people made of *reductio ad absurdum* at a very early time. What does it show? That talk about divinity, by that time, had been reduced to considerations of power. But that is the problem we face – why power *and nothing else*?

The eminent Greek Scholar Gilbert Murray gives us a hint. The ancient gods were local gods. They resided on a local hill or in a local temple and had local idiosyncrasies. Occasionally gods in different places had the same name. There was a Zeus of Dodona and a Zeus on Mount Olympus.

When the Greeks travelled they left their local gods behind, or so it seemed. That was somewhat of a problem. It was not safe to be without your special divinity. On the other hand they encountered gods that were similar to their local gods in some respects, different in others. Naturally, they emphasized and perhaps even noticed only the similarities and disregarded the differences. One might say they were *superficial and forgetful* – they soon forgot the idiosyncrasies of their local gods. One might also say that they *abstracted* from these idiosyncrasies. At any rate, the result was the same. The gods increased in power – they were now more than local gods – and lost in individuality – they were also less than local gods. An acquaintance with alien gods – like the gods of the Persians or of the Egyptians – further smoothed out differences. Gods more and more became big, powerful but faceless bastards.

Now it is interesting to see how eagerly 'philosophers' participated in this collective superficiality and forgetfulness. Moreover, they turned the whole thing around. Omitting specifics, to them, was not a loss but a gain; it brought people closer to what they soon called 'truth' or 'reality'. They therefore not only continued on the path entered by their unphilosophical and forgetful predecessors, they plastered it with invitations called arguments and asserted that they were dealing with the nature of things, not just with changing opinions. I already mentioned some of the arguments which Xenophanes used to ridicule the Homeric gods. Let me now present them to you, in a more verbatim fashion:

> But the mortals consider that the gods were created by birth
> that they wore clothes, had voices and also a form.
> But if cattle, or lions, or horses had hands, just like humans;
> if they could paint with their hands, and draw and thus create
> pictures –
> then the horses in drawing their gods would draw horses;
> and cattle
> would give us pictures and statues of cattle; and therefore
> each would picture the gods to resemble their own constitution.
> Aethiopian gods – snub nosed and black
> Thracians – blue eyed and blond [incomplete]
>
> These are fragments 14, 15, 16
> in the Diels-Kranz numbering.

Here is what some modern writers have said about these lines. Guthrie, who wrote a five-volume history of Greek philosophy, speaks of 'destructive criticism'.[5] Mircea Eliade praises Xenophanes' 'acute criticism'[6] and Karl Popper who regards Xenophanes as one of his (of course, minor) forerunners reads the fragments as the 'discovery that the Greek stories about the gods cannot be taken seriously because they represent the gods as human beings.'[7]

The Abundance of Nature

But is it true that they cannot be taken seriously and that Xenophanes' lines reveal this fact? It depends. Looking at the matter historically we see that the 'destructive criticism' is nothing but an extension of the path of forgetfulness that had already been entered upon. It therefore makes little sense to praise Xenophanes for his inventiveness or his 'creativity', as is the fashion today. On the other hand, assume that some people decide not to be forgetful; that they carefully preserve the memory of their gods and note the differences between them and what they find in other countries. In this case we are dealing with tribal divinities and with believers who are aware of that fact. But now the so-called 'criticism' becomes a correct description of their belief. 'Yes', they might reply to Xenophanes, 'you are right. Our gods are indeed tribal gods, they take care of us and they look like us – after all, we were built in their shape! *And regarding animals*; well, we don't find anything absurd in the idea that they have their gods, too, and that, as artists, they would give them their own shape.' Besides, the fact that the gods are pictured in different human shapes and with different facial features cannot be used to argue that they are inhuman. Just as the fact that pictures of great scientists show white, black, Asian and Indian faces does not show that scientists are inhuman. At any rate, Xenophanes' argument works only if you are already convinced that there are no gods, only abstract principles. But then you don't need the argument anyway.

Let me interrupt the tale at this place and read you a poem by a Nobel Prize Winner, Czeslaw Milosz. Milosz praises Reason and Philosophy. His poem shows what a modern intellectual, a poet even, has made of the ancient, philosophy-driven superficiality I have just described. It also shows how the powers of Reason are being used by some of their foremost defenders. They are used to glorify superficial, ill-informed and inhumane ideas all the while providing the defenders of such ideas with a good conscience and more than a touch of self-righteousness.

Here is the poem (which Milosz himself translated into English)

INCANTATION

Human reason is beautiful and invincible;	1
No bars, no barbed wire, no pulping of books,	
no sentence of banishment can prevail against it.	
It establishes universal ideas in language	
and guides our hand to write Truth and Justice	5
with capital letters, and lie and oppression with small.	
It puts what should be above things as they are	
it is the enemy of despair and the friend of hope.	
It does not know the Jew from Greek or slave from master	
giving us the estate of the world to manage.	10
It saves austere and transparent phrases	
from filthy discord of tortured words.	
It says that everything is new under the sun,	
opens the congealed fist of the past.	
Beautiful and very young are Philo-Sophia	15
and poetry, her ally in the service of the Good.	
As late as yesterday Nature celebrated her birth.	
The news was brought to the mountains by a unicorn and an echo	
Their friendships will be glorious, they have no limit.	
Their enemies have delivered themselves to destruction.[8]	20

'Destruction' (20) threatens the opponents of a non-regional Reason intent on 'manag[ing] the estate of the world' (10) without any 'filthy discord of tortured words' (12), i.e. without democratic discussion. 'Destruction' did indeed remove all those small and well-adapted societies that were in the way of the expansion of Western civilization, even though they tried to defend their rights with 'tortured words'. Nobel reason, on the other hand, is hardly 'invincible' (1); prophets, salesmen, politicians, warriors bent on torture, rape and murder trample it underfoot, the alleged friends of reason distort it to make it fit their intentions. The sciences of the past have showered us with useful and terrible gifts – but without employing a single unchangeable and 'invincible' agency. The sciences of today are business enterprises run on business principles – just remember the haggling about the financing of the human genome project and the Texas supercollider. Research in large institutes is not guided by Truth and Reason but by the most rewarding fashion and the Great Minds of today increasingly turn to where the money is, which for a long time meant military research. Not 'Truth' is taught at our universities, but the opinion of influential schools. Not Reason or Enlightenment, but a firm faith (in the Bible or in Marx) was the strongest preserving force in Hitler's prisons, as Jean Améry discovered.[9] 'Truth' written in 'capital letters' (6) is an orphan in this world, without power and influence and *fortunately* so, for the creature Milosz praises under this name could only lead to the most abject slavery. It cannot stand diverging opinions – it calls them 'lies' (6); it puts itself 'above' (7) the real lives of human beings, demanding, like all totalitarian ideologies, the right to rebuild the world from the height of 'what should be' (7), i.e. in accordance with its own 'invincible' (1) precepts. It fails, even refuses to recognize the many ideas, actions, feelings, laws, institutions, racial features which separate one nation (culture, civilization) from another and which alone give us people, i.e. *creatures with faces* (9). The early philosophers, Xenophanes and Parmenides among them, took individual faces away from the gods and replaced them, by faceless principles. Milosz, the humanitarian, goes one step further. He takes faces away from people and replaces them by a faceless abstract and uniform notion of humanity.

This is the attitude that destroyed Indian cultural achievements in the USA without as much as a glance in their direction; this is the attitude that later destroyed many non-Western cultures under the guise of 'development'. Conceited, self-satisfied and utterly blind is this faith in Truth and Reason for which a democratic discussion is but a 'filthy discord of tortured words' (12) – and also very uninformed: philosophy was never the 'ally' (15) of poetry; not in antiquity when Plato spoke of the 'ancient battle between philosophy and poetry' (*Republic* 607b6f), not today when Truth is sought in the sciences, when poetry is reduced to the expression of feelings and when philosophy is interpreted (by deconstructionists) as a poetry not aware of its true nature. It is amazing how many idiocies can be stuffed into a single poem – it can't

have been 'a unicorn and an echo' that brought 'the news'
– it most certainly was an old and decrepit donkey.

Let me return once more to Xenophanes, who lies at the
beginning of this trend. He was not really that bad. He liked
parties and wrote about them. Naturally, writing about them
he also expressed his ideas – but in an interesting and humane
way, not like Milosz, who sounds like the executive vice
president for public relations in an enterprise called REASON.
So, to rescue poetry, let me now quote a long passage from
one of *his* works. Here it is (fragment B1 in the usual
numbering):

> Clean is the floor; clean are the hands and the cups; and the
>   garlands
> freshly now woven, are put on the heads by the boy.
> Redolent balsam preserved in the phial is brought by another,
> exquisite pleasure lies waiting for us in the bowl;
> and a different wine, with the promise of never bringing
>   displeasure,
> soft-tasting and sweet to the smell, stands here in the jar.
> And in the centre the incense dispenses the holy perfume;
> cool water is there, full of sweetness and clear to the eye.
> Behold the gold yellow loaves and, on the magnificent tables,
> overflowing abundance of cheese and rich honey.
> And in the centre, an altar fully covered with flowers
> and festive songs sounding all over the house.
> But first it is proper for well-disposed men to the gods to pay
>   tribute
> with words which are pure and stories that fit the occasion;
> then, after the common libations and the prayer for the
>   strength to act wisely
> (the most important concern, preceding all others)
> it is not hubris to fill the body with drink – provided
> only the old ones need later a slave to get home.
> And I praise the man who, having imbibed can still remember
> how much he achieved and how he followed the virtues.
> Let him not tell us of battles conducted by Titans and Giants
> or even Centaurs – the fantasies of our fathers;
> or of civic dissension – not useful are these events.
> But one should always pay respect to the gods.

The Abundance of Nature

This poem has a variety of interesting features. First, the surroundings; it is a somewhat restrained party where one thinks of the gods (*NOT* of one single god-monster) and does not drink to excess. While some poets, like Alkaios, praised drinking for its own sake, and while those who imitated the Lydians 'were so corrupted that some of them, being drunk, saw neither the rising nor the setting of the sun' (Athenaios' paraphrase of the end of Xenophanes, fragment 3), Xenophanes advises his drinking companions to drink with moderation so that only the elderly will need a slave to get home. We owe the fragment to precisely these observations: the sophist Athenaeus, who lived in the first century BC, quoted it in his long book on dietetics.

The second interesting feature is the content of the conversations. They are not about wars or Homeric topics; they are about the personal experiences of the participants – 'how much they achieved and how they followed the virtues'. According to Xenophanes these matters are furthered neither by Homer, nor by the modern craze for athletics (which he condemned in another fragment) nor even by personal war stories. A new idea of human excellence announces itself.

Not all early thinkers belonged to the Xenophanes–Parmenides category. In China scientists used a multiple approach corresponding to the many different regions of nature and the variety of her products. There was a unity – but it was a loose connection between events, not an underlying essence. This view was more practical than its Western alternative and indeed, Chinese technology, medicine included, was for a long time far ahead of the West. I say, 'it was far ahead of the West' as if I knew. Well, I don't know. I don't know Chinese. I haven't seen the relevant evidence. I only read a few books, some volumes of Needham's monstrous work on Chinese science included, and this is what they say.[10] When the 'scientific revolutions' of the sixteenth and seventeenth centuries started in the West, Western technology was rather primitive compared with Chinese technology. And this is a great puzzle for many historians: how did it happen that an event that revolutionized technology everywhere, China included, occurred in 'backward' Europe and not in advanced China? Because Europe had an abstract philosophy? And how can an abstract philosophy lead to concrete advances? Perhaps because the so-called 'advances' also introduced new standards and because the new standards regarded as excellent what was regarded as execrable before? So, you see, there are lots of things to think about!

At any rate, even in the West not all philosophers who proposed generalities proposed them in the same way, by relying on forgetfulness. Some philosophers defended generalities by using well-known facts. One of them, Pythagoras, is especially interesting. We can say that he was a scientist. His school made contributions to arithmetic, geometry, astronomy and ethics. The contributions were specific (in arithmetic we have a series of very interesting principles and theorems) as well as general, dealing with the nature of things. Science was not an end in itself. Learning science was a means of purifying the soul. So we have here a doctrine which satisfies the demand for a coherent world view connecting precise scientific matters with the properties of the soul – a very interesting view indeed, and also a very puzzling one.

Some time ago I mentioned the difficulties of identifying the precise views held by ancient philosophers. In many cases the evidence consists of fragments found in later authors who used them for attacking the ancients and who no longer understood what they had intended. Friendly interpreters assumed that all philosophers said more or less the same things and differed in details only. Simplicius, the leading Aristotelian of the sixth century, assumed that Plato and Aristotle agreed in their basic philosophical principles and selected his quotations accordingly. We have every reason to view the evidence they give us and its interpretation with a critical eye. However this evidence was at least real evidence; it came from books that had been written by the philosophers and had been 'published' by them in the sense in which publication was understood in antiquity. The case of Pythagoras is much more difficult. The Pythagorean School

The Abundance of Nature

habitually ascribed all important discoveries to The Great Pythagoras himself. It also reported 'real' events (which, as in the case of Thales, may have been rumours) side-by-side with mythical tales showing, for example, how rivers, animals, even lions recognized Pythagoras, bowed before him and praised him. Major Pythagorean treatises were written long after Pythagoras had died and with the intention of demonstrating his superhuman qualities. Needless to say, Pythagoreanism is a fertile battleground for scholars. I shall tell you what seems to be plausible today. Don't think that this is the last word or the final, uncontested truth; a few years from now the situation may look very different. But it's an interesting story.

Pythagoras started out in Samos, under the tyrant Polycrates. At that time there were many different forms of government, around the Mediterranean, and further inland. There were kingdoms, democracies, oligarchies, tyrannies and others. Tyrants were not always bad. They often got power with the help of the powerless and oppressed. People who had suffered from years of injustice and suppression picked a nobleman as their leader and overthrew the rest of nobility with his help. Tyrants so created might rule benevolently for some time, maybe for their entire lives. Their sons usually lacked their character or their finesse and the situation soon became as bad as it had been before. At any rate, Pythagoras grew up in Samos, a little island ahead of Asia Minor, under the tyrant Polycrates. Having his own political ideas, he didn't get along too well with Polycrates; so he moved to Croton, in southern Italy.

When he arrived he first addressed all the women from Croton; he explained what he thought was the right kind of life for them and for people generally. Next he addressed the young men up to the age of about seventeen and told them – using different words, because being young you listen in a different way – about the nature of society, about their own role in it and about the role of their parents, he talked about the nature of the gods and so on. Finally, he addressed the mature men – the warriors and the politicians. His speeches were so popular that he got elected to a powerful political position in Croton.

This story of Pythagoras' deeds in Croton is almost too incredible to be true. Think about it. This guy, a stranger to the people from Croton, arrives from faraway Samos. Making his speeches he most likely used his own particular dialect which may have sounded to the Crotonites as Bavarian sounds to Prussians, or Sicilian to a Piedmontese. Differences in language usually put a boundary between people, but in his case they didn't.

Next Pythagoras created a political party, but the Crotonians soon found reasons for worry. The party was rather secretive. Joining it was a long drawn-out process. First, years of initial training with little reward to test the constancy and determination of those who had joined. After about five years the candidates could hear the voice of Pythagoras (or was it the voice of a stand-in?), but they could not see him. Remember the movie *The Crimes of Doctor Mabuse*. Dr Mabuse gives the orders – but never in person. He sits behind a screen; only his voice is heard. Later it turns out that he is not even there in person; the orders come from a tape recorder. Well, Pythagoras, apparently, was a little like Dr Mabuse. The Crotonians, eventually, thought so too and they chased the Pythagoreans out of town. Many people were killed. Pythagoras fled to the temple of a goddess; after one version he died there, after another he survived and lived to a ripe old age. And, some modern Pythagoreans might be inclined to think, if he has not died he is still living among us, perhaps in the body of a wise old bulldog.

What did Pythagoras teach? He taught arithmetic, geometry and astronomy. And he taught these subjects as a way to purification and salvation. Again knowledge is not just practical mastery – it has a function over and above mere usefulness. It keeps the soul on the right track.

Let me remind you incidentally that a very modern physicist, Wolfgang Pauli, tried to use knowledge in exactly the same manner. Having been associated with C. G. Jung, the Freudian apostate, he wanted to tie knowledge to matters of the soul. Early scientists, Kepler among them, had divined such a connection and had worked towards it. Pauli wrote an essay on this aspect of Kepler's physics and astronomy. Classical physics, which means nineteenth-century physics, explicitly rejected any connection of this kind. This is what its 'objectivity' was thought to consist in. An approach between physics, psychology and religion, the three subjects into which the older knowledge had split, was impossible. It was no longer excluded by quantum mechanics – and Pauli tried to make the best of this new opportunity. He tried to unite religion, mind and science. Don't think that Pauli was one of those wishy-washy scientists who speak precisely about a narrow domain but become all tears when dealing with the rest. Pauli had an acute, critical mind. As a matter of fact, he was called 'the scourge of physics' because of the way in which he criticized his fellow physicists. Einstein and Bohr spoke to him on equal terms and occasionally received a severe beating. His letters contained not only criticisms, but also positive suggestions and he was not at all averse when, using these suggestions, someone else got a Nobel Prize. The idea of intellectual property seems to have been entirely alien to him – a strange trait in a modern scientist! Anyhow, he soon got a Nobel Prize himself. So, the old Pythagorean idea was not as ridiculous as it may seem to a modern 'enlightened' person. Back to Pythagoras! One of the basic ideas of the Pythagorean philosophy was that everything consisted of units and that these units were numbers. This was a form of atomism, though a very abstract form. And there were some arguments as to why it might be true. The arguments were of two kinds: there existed numerous relations between numbers, i.e. there existed a *theory of numbers*. And numerical relations were found to exist in nature, i.e. the theory was not empty but had *applications*. One of the most astounding applications was in music. There exists an infinite variety of noises. Only a few of these noises are sounds – but sounds still form an infinite variety. Of these special noises again very few stand in harmonic relations to each other and these are characterized by relations between integers: 1/2 – the octave; 2/3 – the fifth; 3/4 – the major third; and so on. At any rate, both the symmetries of the theory and the properties of the applications suggested that all is numbers. This was the first version, in the West, of the idea that science is based on mathematics and that relations are scientific only when they can be expressed in mathematical terms. Considering that mathematics, for the Pythagoreans, was arithmetic and that geometry was thought to be subjected to arithmetical laws (remember the Pythagorean triangles) this meant that according to the Pythagoreans a relation was scientific, or that it expressed knowledge, only when stated in arithmetical terms.

The example of music also illustrates the cosmology of the Pythagoreans. There is a continuity of sounds – but what is rational in it can be expressed in integers. Similarly the Pythagoreans assumed that the cosmos started out as a big cloud out of which discontinuous entities formed. Chaos, i.e. continuity, still hovers at the edges.

Now compare what I have told you so far with Parmenides. Both Pythagoras and Parmenides are very abstract thinkers (I say 'Pythagoras', not 'the Pythagoreans' because that is easier). They look for general laws. But they go about it in different ways. Pythagoras, so it seems, pays attention to existing achievements in mathematics which for him means arithmetic and geometry and to its application (as we would say today – for Pythagoras the two things may not have been separated). He develops his views by generalizing both. Parmenides, whose criticism may have been directed against the Pythagoreans, directs his attention to a basic term of all discourse – to the term 'it is' or *estin* in his poem. Numbers are, water is, everything is, or is Being. From that he derives that the most basic level is without change and difference. It is a static continuum. Note that the idea of a continuum (today we would say of an everywhere dense set) i.e. of an entity that is the same between any two of its parts (abstractly considered) originates here, with Parmenides. Aristotle's theory of the continuum is a development of Parmenides, applied to geometry and motion. It has the interesting consequence that a moving body has no well-defined length. At any rate, here we have two scientists – we may well call them that – who, arguing in different ways, introduce ideas that played a large role later on and are still playing an important role.

Now I want to show you something. It is a theorem that can be found in Euclid but is of much older origin. How do we know that? From the language and the way of arguing. We can also say that it is Pythagorean. Why? Because it uses the alternative even-odd as a basis of the argument. This alternative played a large role in Pythagorean philosophy – it was part of a much larger table of opposites including male (odd)-female (even), right-left – and so on. Professor Seidenberg, who has been examining the origins of mathematical concepts and procedures and who discovered a primitive layer, where numbers were arranged in pairs, conjectured that counting derives from a primitive rite involving pairs in a continuing dance.[11] That would explain how even and odd came to be associated with female and male and why the Pythagoreans retained this association in their table of opposites. Well, so far the background, and now the theorem.

If you have a square, then the square over the diagonal is twice as large as the square itself. If you have a good drawing (which mine is not) you can see that immediately.

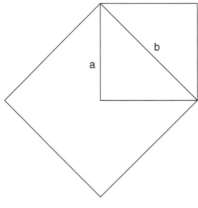

Thus $b^2 = 2a^2$.

Now omit any common factors on both sides. Then the equation tells you that b is even and that a is odd. (Remember we have omitted the common factors!) This means that b can be written in the form 2c. Every even number can be written in this form. Now with $b = 2c$, we get $4c^2 = 2a^2$, then $2c^2 = a^2$ and then, by the argument used before, we get that a is even. Thus a is both even and odd – we have a contradiction. What went wrong? The assumption that the side and the diagonal or, more generally, that the lengths of lines can always be expressed in integers.

Now imagine the effect this discovery must have had on some early Pythagoreans! They assumed that everything consists of numbers and that knowledge expresses relations between numbers – when speaking of numbers I always mean integers, one, two, three, four – not things like *pi* or the square root of two. Now there is an entity that certainly belongs to science, the diagonal of a square, and it cannot be expressed in terms of integers. What would a similar situation be today? That some important scientific facts cannot be expressed mathematically! It would be a disaster.

And there are indeed various stories that tell us that it was regarded as a disaster. For example there is the story that the Pythagoreans wanted to keep the discovery a secret. But one of them could not keep his mouth shut. He was severely punished. Two generations later, however, the proof had become commonplace. Plato mentions it in his dialogue *Theateitos*; he uses it as an example for showing something entirely different; he does not make any fuss about the case – square roots and their incommensurability with the unit have become commonplace. Scientists have learned how to deal with them. Today one would say that the concept of a number was extended to cover entities which, though not integers, yet obeyed most of the laws of integers. Later on mathematicians invented new disciplines and gradually they covered practically all reasoning. Even the statement that mathematics is a purely quantitative science is not true any longer. There is set theory, there is topology. Thus the statement that everything can be expressed in a mathematical manner has now almost become a tautology.

Discussion

QUESTION: We have now seen a proof that the square root of 2 is an irrational number. Proving that the square root of 2 is an irrational number implies that the square root of 2 cannot be explained as a relation between integers.

Let's assume that a and b are two integers, then we prove that this leads to an absurdity. As a conclusion, the square root of two is an irrational number. Where's the problem?

FEYERABEND: Of course, there is no problem today. Today we know integers, fractions, irrational numbers, transcendent numbers, we know transfinites and so on. When the proof was first suggested all that was known was integers. And integers were thought to be the essence of things, at least of all rational things. Now the diagonal of a square which seemed to be an eminently rational matter could not be represented by an integer, when compared with the side. Given the background that meant that it could not be represented by numbers at all. Those who thought everything could be represented by numbers were in great trouble. The trouble was solved by extending the number concept. But that was a difficult matter – just remember that the first definition of irrational numbers that satisfied modern mathematicians was given by Dedekind, in the nineteenth century.

Let me stay a little longer with these ancient thinkers and let me go even further back – right into Homer. This is dangerous territory, for lots of things are quite unsettled here. I'll start from something that seems more or less safe, at least to me, who does not study the scholarly literature as it evolves from week to week.

Most concepts that are being used in the epics are aggregate concepts; they characterize a thing or a virtue or a situation by enumerating some of its major features. The honour of a person, for example is constituted by his position at the council, in war, by his deeds during battle, by the spoils he receives when the battle is over, and so on. The passage I want to talk about is a speech by Achilles. Agamemnon took away part of his spoils. Achilles left the battle in a rage. Some Greeks, led by Odysseus, tell him that his wrongs have been corrected and that he should return to battle. The wrongs had indeed been corrected, according to the relevant concepts – all the items on the list 'honour' are present. Still, Achilles hesitates. And he explains his hesitation in a long speech where he distinguishes between the list and 'real honour'. In a way, that makes as little sense as distinguishing between a marriage ceremony and a 'real marriage'. Taken seriously it introduces a break between what people think and do and a 'reality' that goes its own way. Good people may suffer, 'bad' people may be rewarded – not only now and then, but because of the way in which the world is built: the universe of Sophocles already announces itself. So it does – but how did Achilles get this idea? His visitors are puzzled, they do not understand him, scholars writing millennia later comment on the 'incommensurability' between this idea and tradition, and all the time the puzzle remains: How could Achilles leave language and yet remain within language – or was he becoming inarticulate? Was he just babbling? And if the latter then what events were needed to turn his inarticulation into sense, for sense it became a few generations later. A few generations later it was quite natural to assume that the domain of human action and human knowledge is not the only domain there is; that there is a 'deeper reality'; that it is rather hidden but that some gifted individuals can find out about it and that the rest must follow. This was a popular view with Plato, it is a popular view today so, if Achilles, in stating the distinction had left language and had become inarticulate, how come that the distinction became basic later on? This, I think, is a very important question which, it seems to me, is closely connected with the rise, first, of 'rationality' and then of science. What is the answer?

The Abundance of Nature

Well, as far as I am concerned, the answer is that the concepts of a language are ambiguous in a rather drastic way: one can change them in a manner that violates basic linguistic rules (assuming these rules are stable and nailed down) without stopping to speak, explain and argue. One can start talking nonsense and, having produced a sufficient amount of it, be praised as the discoverer of a new and profound sense. Physics is full of events of this kind. Planck's quantum theory contained the equation $E = h/T$, where E was the energy of a particle, i.e. of a localized entity and $1/T$ the frequency of a wave process which, in the case of well-defined energy would be infinitely long. 'We all were dumbfounded by this situation,' wrote Wolfgang Pauli, one of the most critical and most imaginative physicists of his time. Formally, the equation was quite useful; it led to correct predictions. But what did it mean?

Today, with quantum mechanics so far advanced, the question is still being asked. The usefulness remains; there also exists an interpretation which is accepted by many scientists. It is not accepted by all and it has its problems, which means that the problem of meaning is still with us. It has not been solved. But has it ever been solved with any concept? Has it been 'solved' with, say, the concept of love? Is there a definition of love, or a poem or a sociological essay that makes love 'entirely clear'? And would such clarity be desirable? Would it be desirable to know, or to think that one knows everything about love? Would that not mean that the matter of love is a closed book and that no further exploration is needed? And what about virtue? The notion certainly has an instrumental function – it feeds into the law which is not absolutely clear but certainly clearer than the existing philosophical effusions about virtue. But there is a feedback effect and both sides can change. The conclusion to which I have come with all these considerations is that language is ambiguous, that it is good that it is ambiguous and that any attempt to nail it down would be the end of thinking, loving, acting, in short, of living. And the fact that some scientists think they have nailed things down while still coming up with revolutionary discoveries and that science students are trained to be precise in a very narrow sense and have to catch up with ambiguity later on only shows to what extent we are ruled by ideology and how little attention we pay to the principles we are ready to explain and defend at the drop of a hat. We are deceived by ideology and deceive it in turn. Let a philosopher figure out that conundrum!

Back to Achilles! Achilles, using the ambiguity of language, impressed on it a new aspect of virtue. We cannot say that he 'revealed' that aspect. That assumes that the aspect was already there and that means that the old side of the ambiguous phenomenon 'virtue' would have to be gone forever. But it was not gone forever! It was kept alive by the sophists, by the common people, by later Homeric singers, and it is being kept alive today by ethical relativists. Where did Achilles get the idea? Not from his creativity. Grand divisions of the kind he introduced in his nonsensical way already existed – between gods and humans and their respective actions, ideas, attitudes. The idea that the gods might rig fortune in the way suggested by Achilles was not so far-fetched and it needed only a foul temperament – and Achilles had that – and some adverse events to make Achilles think accordingly. Now remember that story! Remember the whole affair of Achilles, remember what it suggests about the ambiguity of language and of all phenomena when somebody wants to tell you that science, unambiguously and without any doubt, has established that – and here insert whatever science-freaks want to put over on you.

QUESTION: I want to go back to the question you posed to us on the first day. You spoke of the Cultural Revolution brought about by the first philosophers who disrupted the unitary world view expressed by epic poems, by Aeschylus' tragedy and so on. The question was, is this Cultural Revolution good or not? I think we all agree that it was not good . . . of course it's a question – a position. If we accept that it wasn't good, we should look for a way to re-attain the lost harmony, the lost unity. And this way cannot be –

trying to express some suggestions I had in these days – the way of philosophy (broadly speaking, I mean philosophy as an abstraction, as we spoke of in these days) because philosophy promotes unity on a principle of reason to the prejudice of other aspects of human life and activities, such as emotions, feelings, experience (why not) and so on.

Aeschylus' tragedy seems to offer and to suggest a better solution, overcoming conflicts, the disconnection, by means of a dialectic unity, reaching a dialectic equilibrium which is never static. This is one consideration I wanted to make.

Now, yesterday you pointed out that scientific theories can be considered as mere instruments for useful prediction, for technological application and so on, without necessarily feeling bound to accept the world view (the ontology) implied by those theories. As a matter of fact I often found myself sharing this perspective in my studies, but there is a problem that arose to me in these days, making me feel rather confused. Doesn't this amount to accepting some kind of separateness, again of disconnection, between scientific knowledge (which after all, as a human activity just like any other, is a part of our lives) and world views (which are human products too, a part of our lives as well)?

I don't mean to say that we should accept the world view of science. Perhaps it is preferable and more realistic to imagine that things go the other way round, that is to say, with world view influencing science. But somehow I feel that maybe some attempt should be made in favour of a dialectical recomposition of the two.

In other words, I don't feel completely satisfied with the suggestion to consider scientists as our slaves. And perhaps analogous considerations could be made as regards to philosophy, poor philosophy: throwing it in the garbage seems to me a bit too much.

What do you think about this?

FEYERABEND: To start with, I would not say that the philosophers' appeal to unifying principles and Plato's critique of tragedy, for example, were bad things. Plato's critique led to Aristotle's wonderful essay, which like everything wonderful had good and bad effects.

As regards to the separation of science and poetry, well, to start with, the subjects are separated from each other, and have been separated for quite some time.

Ancient Greek artisans knew things – how to build houses, how to make jewellery, how to heal – which the other citizens did not know. Specialists of this kind are found in all cultures and at all times. They existed in ancient Egypt, in Babylon, in China. The question is what was the social position of these groups?

In Greece many artisans were slaves. Not all of them minded being slaves. As opposed to free men they did not have to go to war. Somewhere in Aristophanes there are tired warriors coming back from the war and what do they find? Rich and happy slaves parading their riches in public.

Aeschylus and Aristophanes were not slaves; still they were different from the common citizens because of their special talent for playwriting: in this respect, they were separated from the other people. For Plato, however, they were not only useless but also dangerous – he wanted to throw them out of his perfect society. Now one problem is: What's the best way of integrating special people like artisans or tragedians into a society? Applied to modern states – what's the best way of dealing with scientists?

I don't think this problem can be solved once and for all. Today we have something like academic freedom. The research and the teaching done by the professors is to be judged by them, not by outside agencies. Many intellectuals regard academic freedom as a basic right and as a holy commandment to be obeyed by the rest of society. But that is a silly attitude to take. The so-called 'right' arose in special historical circumstances when some princes wanted to protect their scientists from the Church. The Church then controlled a large deal of intellectual life and it was important to have a counterforce. Today the shoe is on the other foot; now we need a counterforce against scientific power play. Besides, princes have gone out of fashion, the churches, at least in Western countries, have only a fraction of the power they used to have and democracies, republics have replaced kingdoms. A democracy leaves important matters to the people or their elected representatives. Education is an important matter; so is the way in which large amounts of tax money are being spent. Academic freedom now is as out of place in society at large as the doctrine of the Virgin Birth of Christ would be in a biology classroom. Scientists are either public servants – this they are in state universities – or private employees. In the first case they have an obligation to the state first, to their own manias only in the second place. In the second case, they have to adapt to the programs, the trends and the fashions of the industry in which they work. They may get people around to accepting their ideas – but they have to try; they cannot take it for granted that one will listen to them just because they can fill the blackboard with strange symbols. They may have their own ideas about truth and method and may feel rather strongly about them. Then they write books about these ideas and speak about them on street corners – it's a free country, as some people say (rather optimistically, I believe). But it would be silly to allow them to pound these ideas into the heads of the young to the exclusion of everything else and it would be equally silly to give their suggestions on tricky matters precedence over all other suggestions.

So far I have been talking about the role of special people in society. Should they have privileges, should they be treated like the rest and what is to be done with their inventions? Another problem is how their ideas are to be related to the rest. For example, what is to be the relation between science and religion? Again my answer is that this has to be decided from case to case, it cannot be decided once and for all. Besides, the idea manufacturers are already working on the problem – as a matter of fact they have been working on it since times immemorial. So my suggestion would be just one more suggestion and I am not at all sure it would be new. All you can do is look at what has been done, in the way you find most comfortable or most rewarding and then come to your own conclusion.

QUESTION: In the beginning you pointed out to us that it is very dangerous to unify apparently identical concepts. Sometimes it is a result of superficiality and one loses a lot of particular aspects which are different. Let's talk about atomism, a theory which has been proven and disproven in various periods, so that Democritus' atomism has something to do with twentieth-century atomism.

FEYERABEND: It does have something to do with it, although very little. The connecting element is the assumption that systems have parts and that the behaviour of the whole can be explained by laws that apply to the parts. The difference is that modern atoms or, rather, elementary particles differ from the atoms of Democritos and that the parts cannot be assumed to pre-exist in the system that decays into them.

4

Dehumanizing Humans

In the first lecture I talked about the difference between events that occur in different fields – in astronomy, for example, and in the lives of people in ghettos, or in countries torn apart by wars. On the one side, cool, objective judgement surrounded by pleasure (or disgust), yes, but allegedly not constituted by it. On the other, pain, suffering, the wish for peace frustrated by nationalism and ideological manias. Philosophers have found wonderful ways of showing, not only why there *is no* connection but even why there *should not be* any connection. Science, they say, deals with facts, and these just *are*. Politics, whether of a humane or of a bestial kind, deals with what should be, and there is no way of arguing, in a logically satisfactory way from what is to *what should be* (or vice versa). Moreover, pain and pleasure are not in the things themselves, they are the way in which people react to their surroundings whose true nature is independent of, and unaffected by, these reactions. This is how some philosophers and some philosophically inclined scientists try to justify the various chasms that seem to divide our lives.

But how did the idea of the chasms arise in the first place? Was it a result of 'objective' research and, if so, how did this research get started? There existed a time when natural events were in the hands either of collections of gods or of a single, all-powerful divine being and could be changed by divine will. At any rate, experience showed not a trace of eternal and objective laws. Even Aristotle says that what is natural occurs always or almost always. There were the seasons, true, and the rising and the setting of the sun. But there were also storms, halos, triple suns, earthquakes, comets, meteors, volcanic eruptions: there was rain, hail, the rainbow. Human beings might go off their rocker and run amok while animals occasionally gave birth to monsters. After a cold night the sun brought warmth and life to nature and it was perceived and described as doing that: the physical warmth and the warmth of feeling, gratitude and joy were inextricably connected, both in the phenomena and in the language used for describing them. Even today we speak of a warm feeling for a person or of a cold-hearted bastard. Philosophers of an objectivistic inclination point out that these are vague analogies and that no objective content must be ascribed to the phrase. But the separation did not exist in Homer and Hesiod and is still utilized by poets. This being the case – where were the 'objective facts' to support an 'objective' chasm between nature and feelings? And while nature was being viewed as a dwelling place of the gods – where were the 'objective facts' to indicate that nature, life included, had nothing divine to it, but was nothing but a rather complicated mechanism? You cannot find what is not there, and if you insist that it is there, then you are fantasizing, not doing research. But if the former, where do the fantasies come from?

Remember Monod? He defends objectivism, the idea, that nature knows no purpose. Objectivism, he says, has not been accepted – it is too different from the views of many people. However, it commands attention because of its 'prodigious power of performance'. That it certainly does, among intellectuals at least. But this 'prodigious power of performance' was not there from the beginning. On the contrary; in the early centuries of Greek development, at the time of the Homeric epics, for example, things seemed to run in an entirely different way. How then did 'objectivism' or materialism, to use a more widespread term, arise? And how did it manage to survive without any useful products whatsoever? Useful products, after all, were produced by artisans, not by the followers of Democritos and artisans held on to tradition. So we have here a philosophy that is entirely up in the air and yet survives and millennia later shows a 'prodigious power of performance'. Are there ideas which have similar features?

There are. Christianity is an example. Throughout its existence Christianity had to fight tremendous obstacles. There were the persecutions. Then the world itself seemed to refute the idea of a benign and all-powerful god. There were plagues, wars, thunderstorms; winters might last forever while droughts during the summer wiped out all means of survival. Gangs of robbers and 'legitimate' armies invaded villages, killed the men, raped the women, set fire to their houses – the Thirty Years' War was full of such events. Yet the belief lasted, became even stronger and guided people through their misfortune. Materialism did not offer any consolation. What it offered, at most, was the idea that death was the end of life, not the beginning of, possibly, eternal punishments. Yet it survived, not among the masses, but among small groups of the so-called 'educated' until it was safe, because of its 'prodigious power of performance'. It introduced the gulf between subjective events and objective processes; it was not based on it. But where did this idea come from? What was the origin, the source, the inspiration for an idea which in the end de-anthropomorphized even humans? How did it happen that nature was gradually dehumanized until humans themselves were no longer viewed in a humane way?

Turn now to the sciences as they present themselves today. They are free of values, it is said. But that is simply not so. An experimental result or an observation becomes a scientific fact only when it is clear that it does not contain any 'subjective' elements – that it can be detached from the process that led to its announcement. This means that values play an important role in the constitution of scientific facts. I meet a friend. In a way I see our whole relationship written in her face. She looks now different from the way she looked to me when I first met her and she will look different again a few years from now. This look is not an objective fact. It does not sit on her face waiting to be discovered by an objective experimental procedure. It is part of our relationship and it involves me in an essential way. It is therefore not a scientific fact though it is more important to me than any scientific fact could ever be. However, it is not 'scientifically important' and if science takes over, not socially important either. Is it not clear that science and values are intertwined in a complex and not always transparent way? And that the separation between subjects which exists today cannot simply be removed by an act of will?

It is this situation which lies behind my way of dealing with problems which today are classified as 'philosophical'. It often happens to me that having told a story such as the story of Thales, or the story of Xenophanes, people ask for a 'systematic account'. A story, they think, is nice – but it is also rather superficial. It does not get to the root of the matter. For example, I can tell you a story as to how certain views about the nature of knowledge arose. However, this does not answer the question what knowledge is. To answer this question we have to proceed 'systematically' by using principles and logic. But where do the principles and the logic come from? And why should we use their present version and not an earlier version, or a version cherished by a different culture, or by a different philosophical school? Experience and experiment decide, says a modern slogan. And why? Because that's how things are done today. And why should an existing practice be taken as our guide? After all, there are still other procedures around. Because experience and experiment have been successful. Successful at what? Successful at bringing peace, or at making people more loving? Not a chance! They were successful at finding general laws which in turn led to interesting technologies. Did they find these general laws by experimental procedures?

Dehumanizing Humans

No – because these procedures were used only later in the history of the West. They arose when the idea of general laws had as yet no empirical foundation. Does this mean that even today we can pursue views without an empirical foundation? Apparently it does. At any rate, all these problems can be clarified (not solved!) by taking a look at history. I do not mean to say that history is the answer while a systematic approach is not. There is no 'the' answer. History is only a first step towards making this discovery. It undermines previous certainties and raises problems for principles that seemed to be well-established – but it is not itself a new and better foundation. What is? I really do not know. As a matter of fact I think that there is no way of finding a 'foundation' or a form of discourse which is superior to everything else. So for the time being, let me continue with my story of the situation in ancient (i.e. ninth to fifth century BC) Greece.

There existed various groups. There were the Homerides, i.e. the singers who continued the tradition of Homer. They earned an income by going from one place to another and reciting their songs – wherever they arrived they were fed and housed. 'Sixty-seven years have now been carrying my meditations through the land of Greece . . . ,' writes Xenophanes. Then there were common people, the nobility, there were artisans (slaves many of them) and there were the philosophers. To begin with they did not form a special group. Thales, Parmenides, Plato were rich citizens who participated or intended to participate in the political life of their cities. They were not yet professionals, 'philosophers'. The situation changes in the fifth century, when the sophists arrived.

Ever since Aristophanes and Plato, the sophists have had bad press. They were accused of being superficial: they took money for their troubles; they misguided the young, it was said, told them how to cheat and, to add insult to injury, how to argue that they had done the right thing. There is a marvellous dialogue by Plato, a farce, almost, the *Euthydemus*, which reveals some aspects of their activity. The scene is the Lykeion, one of the three known gymnasia of classical

96

Athens. Gymnasia had arrangements for athletics, washing rooms and dressing rooms where one could sit and talk. Socrates is alone in the dressing room and about to leave. He gets one of his presentiments – an inner voice tells him to remain, so he sits down again. In come Euthydemus and Dionysodorus surrounded 'by a number of pupils, I think', says Socrates, who is telling the story. They walk around two or three times, when they are joined by Clinias and, behind him, a group of his admirers – love between men and love of men for young boys was quite customary at the time. Ctesippus, a fine handsome young man but quite wild as young men are, is among them. Clinias sees Socrates, comes towards him, sits down on his right side (I am mentioning the details because some of you might want to produce the dialogue as a play, either verbatim, or with a changed text). Socrates was ugly, frog-faced, as he called himself, but he had great charm, young men (including Plato) felt attracted to him. So there is Socrates, sitting with Clinias on his right side. Euthydemus and Dionysodorus notice them, look at them, look back at each other, look at them again and finally come up to them, Euthydemus sitting down at Clinias' right and Dionysodorus at Socrates left. Good day, says Socrates and introduces Dionysodorus and Euthydemus to Clinias: 'They are wise men: they know everything about war, as much as is needed for becoming a general, all about tactics, how to lead an army, how to fight in full armour and they know also how to defend oneself in a law court.'

Teachers of fighting had existed before; gradually the activity became professionalized. Law courts were an old institution. There is a law court on the famous shield of Achilles in the *Iliad* (Book XVIII, 503ff). The accused had to defend themselves in person, often about military matters. They had no lawyers. But they were advised by more experienced people. This activity of advising also became slowly professionalized. Socrates knew that Dionysodorus and Euthydemus had been professional advisers in the art of war and in law suits – and he informed Clinias to that effect.

Dehumanizing Humans

But 'they turned up their noses at this; they looked at each other and laughed and Euthydemus said: "We don't deal with these matters any longer – we just treat them as side shows."'

'You surprise me,' said Socrates, 'your main show must be a fine one if such great subjects have come to be side shows; so, in heaven's name tell me what this show is about!'

'Virtue, Socrates! And we believe we can teach it, faster and better than anyone else in the world!'

Virtue was indeed one of the subjects taught by the sophists, by lesser ones, and by great sophists such as Protagoras. Socrates challenges Euthydemus and Dionysodorus to demonstrate their art. 'Persuade this young man, Clinias, that he must love wisdom and practise virtue!'

During this exchange Euthydemus leaned forward and Ctesippus who was eager to hear and to be close to Clinias could not see him any longer. So he got up, and placed himself right in front of Clinias and Socrates. The others, the followers of Euthydemus and Dionysodorus as well as the admirers of Clinias, did the same and surrounded Socrates, Clinias, Euthydemus and Dionysodorus. Imagine this situation; put it vividly before your eyes and you will get a flavour not only of this particular dialogue, but of a tiny little part of public life in ancient Athens. Euthydemus begins with the performance.

'Now, Clinias,' he says, 'which are the people who learn – the wise ones, or the ignorant ones?'

This was a large question, (Socrates continues his report). The boy blushed and looked at me in doubt. 'Cheer up, dear Clinias', I said, 'and answer like a man.'

Just then Dionysodorus leaned over to me and whispered in my ear, smiling all over his face: 'Now pay attention, Socrates – whatever the lad answers, he will be refuted.'

I had no chance to warn the boy, for he gave his answer right then, while Dionysidorus spoke and he said that it was the wise ones that learned.

And Euthydemus continued, 'There are people you call teachers, are there not?'

He agreed.

'The teachers teach those who learn; for example the – music master and the grammar master were teachers of you and the other boys and you learned?'

He said, 'Yes.'

'Of course, when you were learning you did not yet know the things you were learning?'

'No', he said.

'Then you were wise when you did not know these things?'

'Certainly not', said he.

'If not wise, then ignorant?'

'Yes.'

'So you boys, while learning what you did not know, were ignorant?'

The boy nodded.

'So the ignorant learn, my dear Clinias, not the wise as you suppose.'

And when he said this it was like conductor and chorus; he signalled and they all cheered and laughed. Euthydemus, Dionysodorus and their followers. Then before the boy could even catch his breath Dionysodorus took over and said – what happened, my dear Clinias, when the grammar man dictated to you? Which of the boys learned the things dictated – the wise or the ignorant?

'The wise ones,' said Clinias.

'Then the wise ones learn, not the ignorant, and you answered wrong just now to my brother.'

Then indeed the two-men entourage laughed loud and long, applauding their wisdom. But all the rest of us were dumb struck and did not know what to say.

This little scene has various interesting features. First, it presents two men who changed their profession in mid-life – they became teachers of 'virtue'. Secondly, it shows part of their repertory, namely, arguments leading to paradoxical conclusions. Those confronted with the arguments are 'dumb-struck and do not know what to say'. Such arguments were not only used for entertainment. Offered before a law court they could defeat an opponent. Thirdly, this very danger made some sophists examine the matter in some detail: doing this they prepared what today is known as logic with its distinction between valid and invalid reasoning. Fourth, we learn that paradoxes were debated publicly and that the debate had an interested audience: people were interested in logical matters. Even during the so-called Dark Ages, some Saints staged debates with dissenters and won the debates with their superior reasoning. Right now, however, we are in the middle of paradox.

'My dear Ctesippus – do you really think it is possible to tell a lie?'

'Yes by heaven – or I am nuts.'

'In making the statement so-called, or in not making it?'

'In making it', he replied (again Socrates is speaking – he reports what happened when he remained in the anteroom of the gymnasium).

'In that case – when he makes the statement, is he not talking about something different from what he actually says?'

'How could he?' said Ctesippus.

'Clearly, then, what he is talking about is something different from other things.'

'Sure.'

'Therefore, when making his statement, he is talking about it.'

'Yes.'

'Now then, talking about it, he states it as it is and speaks the truth?'

'Yes', said Ctesippus, 'but he that makes these statements, Euthydemus, is not speaking about things as they are.'

'Then,' Euthydemus went on, 'surely the things that are not are not!'

'They are not.'

'And the things that are not can only be nowhere.'

'OK.'

'Is it possible then that anyone, I don't care who he is, could do something about these things that are not so as to make them to be the things that are nowhere?'

'I don't think so,' said Ctesippus.

'Very well; when the orators speak in public – do they do nothing?'

'Oh no – they are doing something.'

'Then if they do, they also make?'

'Yes.'

'Then to speak is both to do and to make?'

He agreed.

'Then', said he, 'no one ever says the things that are not, for he would at once make them something . . . 'and so on. In a similar way Euthydemus and Dionysodorus argue that there is no way of contradicting somebody. The first party says what he says, the second party says what he says, the two things are different, each one speaks about his own subject matter – and that is that. Nor are there any false opinions, for everyone says what he says – and that is that. The background of all these arguments is Parmenides as changed by Protagoras. According to Parmenides you cannot say what is not – saying what is not is the same as not saying anything. At any rate, the sophists were the first to bring these difficulties out into the open, into the law courts, into public debates, and in the course of time slowly built up the subject of rhetoric and the related subject of logic. Remember, this was the time of total democracy. Every free citizen (that still excluded slaves, foreigners and women – note incidentally, that most sophists were foreigners!) sooner or later would chair the public assembly, or speak in it. Or they would have to defend themselves in a law court – they had to speak for themselves, they could not let a lawyer speak for them. The art of making a good speech was an old art. The Homeric warriors were supposed to excel in battle and in the art of making a good speech. The sophists made a science out of this art and examined the nature of language. From there they wandered off into other subjects and, finally, dealt with everything under the sun. Hippias, for example, boasted that everything he wore had been designed and made by himself. He made contributions to mathematics and had speeches ready on almost every subject: short and inexpensive speeches for modest occasions, medium and more expensive speeches for parties and long and very expensive speeches for special occasions.

Needless to say the knowledge produced by the sophists, though 'sophisticated', lacked depth. In a sense this was progress – deep knowledge creates deep respect and deadens our critical abilities. The sophists, we might say, led people out of a religious approach to knowledge into a more mundane approach. This was an advantage, but not entirely so. Already Plato realized that life without some kind of commitment is bound to be rather shallow. He despised the sophists because of their shallowness and because they took money (he could do this easily; after all, he was independently wealthy) – but there were exceptions. Protagoras and Gorgias, he always mentions with respect. Nor was he too happy about the idea that good arguments could be found for any cause and that it was possible 'to turn the weaker case into the stronger'. This is what Protagoras seems to have believed – and here he hit upon an interesting and, to some people, rather disturbing problem, namely, that ingenuity can find a good defence for almost any position. Life, after all, is very complicated. It has features which usually remain hidden but can be called forth by an ingenious argument. The argument, though 'rational', may not achieve its aim, namely, to turn people around – which shows that reason alone is not a sufficient guide to life. There are other factors. Plato has very interesting things to say about this situation.

How did Plato get into philosophy? He answers this question in his *seventh letter*. As you know Plato wrote dialogues. This was a conscious decision on his part. A writer trying to tell a story or to present ideas had various styles at his disposal. The *epic style* was the oldest. Homer for a long time was the only source of information about history, the gods and the virtues. Revolutionaries like Xenophanes and Parmenides still used the hexameter to explain their views. *Lyric poetry* introduced different types of verse and addressed different problems. Most lyric poets spoke in a personal way; some of them made fun of ancient customs. The *drama* combined argument, sight and sound to show the consequences of certain ways of living. Aeschylus, for example, can be regarded as an ancient Piscator – much simpler, of course, but by no means less impressive.[1] Plato and Aristotle wrote essays about the tragic mode of presentation, the first attacking it (in Book X of the *Republic*) the second formulating an ingenious defence (in his *Poetics*). Neither of them does justice to what actually happened on the stage. The *Oresteia* of Aischylos, for example, has little in common with what Aristotle says about tragedy.

Then there was the new medium of *scientific prose* which started in Ionia and spread from there all over Greece. Of course, people had been talking prose all the time, but scientific prose was as different from their daily exchanges as is a modern article about bees from the language of beekeepers. Herodotus, in his *Histories,* uses a mixture of styles, including the novel, the short story, the one-liner, the instructive example and, of course, scientific prose. Plato analysed the styles – and he rejected all of them. In this he showed much greater freedom than modern philosophers who don't even consider the problem, who get upset when serious matters are being presented in a disrespectful or in a dramatic way, and who at any rate are being controlled by editors with their own ideas about the proper shape of a philosophical (scientific, theological) sentence. Plato chose the *dialogue*, a new form that had been introduced a little before his own time. His reason which he explains in the *Phaidros* is that the dialogue resembles a personal conversation which, he thought, was the best medium for exploring difficult problems. Of course a written dialogue is not a conversation – it is an artefact; it is the frozen image of part of a conversation and useful only to the participants. Reading the dialogue they are reminded of what happened – which is much more than can ever be written down. For us who live centuries after Plato and Socrates and who never saw their faces, heard their voices or marvelled at their gestures, the dialogues are like scores for musical performances lacking information about the instruments, the mode of playing them, the speed, loudness, nature of the permitted (or required) variations – and so on. They are dead letters which we can revive as we are trying to revive Babylonian compositions but whose original meaning we shall never reach. Plato was aware of the situation. Many of his dialogues contain introductions which make it clear that the real event happened long ago and is remembered by only a few. And in the *Seventh Letter* he says quite explicitly that 'there is no work by Plato and there never will be one.'

Apart from the dialogues Plato also wrote letters. Or, to be more precise, there exist letters said to have been written by Plato which some scholars call genuine while others declare them to be fakes. (This problem also arises with the dialogues, but to a lesser degree.) One letter, the seventh, is accepted by almost all scholars. It tries to justify Plato's actions in Sicily. You see – Plato did not only *write* about politics, he also tried to *realize* the ideal society he had described in his *Republic* – and he failed. The seventh letter explains how he got interested in politics and why he thought that only a new way of thinking about the gods, the physical world, the social world and the nature of humans could overcome the irrationality and the sheer madness of traditional politics.

I shall now explain an aspect of this way which became an important ingredient of Western science and philosophy. Mind you, I shall not discuss the aspect in the form in which it appears in Plato. Plato was an unusual author who often changed his views without indicating that he had done so. The idea I shall describe does play a role in his thought – but it soon took on a life of its own. It inspired scientific work, created philosophical movements and lubricated the many popular enterprises, fashions, study programs, slogans that live off the achievements of both. Put in simple terms the idea has to do with the way in which concepts are being introduced, changed and justified.

Take a concept such as the concept of a tree, or the concept of a human being. Concepts like these arise in a rather intuitive fashion, as a result of having encountered, observed and acted upon many different individuals. The words associated with them and the simple explanations in which they occur convey only part of their content. The remainder resides in the senses which have either adapted to the relevant features or have been trained to perceive them, in the memory which recognizes the features when they return, in the motor apparatus, facial muscles included, which initiate the proper movements, in short, it resides in many parts of the body that understands the concept.

The concept of illness as formed by practical physicians has the same general features but is much more complex. It is kind of a collection bag that assembles many different disturbances and unites them under a single name – 'illness'. The nature and the size of the collection depends on what counts as a normal life and on the character of the disturbances selected. Invasions by belligerent tribes are disturbances – but they are only rarely classified as an illness. Thus the 'nature of illness' depends on the ways in which people organize their affairs, which means that different cultures suffer from different types of illnesses. Curious people then establish connections between the overt aspects of a particular disturbance and more hidden processes and try to discover how the disturbance changes over time – when it is left alone, when it is interfered with by the weather, by the behaviour of friends and family, by changes of the diet or by the actions of a physician. Again most of the knowledge involved is visual, or auditory, or habitual. Those who study the disturbances have to learn *seeing* the relevant aspects, recognizing the 'normal' as well as the 'disturbed' reactions of a human body and adapting their behaviour, perceptions included, to new, unexpected and, to the unprepared, invisible phenomena. They are like artists who, looking at common things, discover unusual properties and represent them in unusual ways. The knowledge they acquire has much in common with the knowledge of athletes, pianists and circus performers. It resides in their body or those parts of their mind that activate the body and it must be communicated by examples and action – words do not suffice. The physical chemist Michael Polanyi called such knowledge 'tacit knowledge'.[2]

Most crafts were and still are based on tacit knowledge. It needs a sure hand and a discerning eye to be an expert jeweller. It also needs a sure hand and a discerning eye to be a good physician – but the vision and the actions required are different in both cases. Everyday concepts such as the concept of anger are tied to a rich reservoir of actions, perceptions, feelings and receive their content from it. The reservoir changes with every new experience and the concepts change with it: the kitchen of a newly bought house looks very different from the same kitchen twenty years later – even if physically it remained the same and the behaviour of the users changes accordingly (the same applies to the husband, the wife, the lover or the mistress that came with the kitchen). Still, definitions, i.e. short sequences of words connecting one common sense concept with another, do have their use – they temporarily link some of the collection bags that constitute our tacit knowledge. They do not replace them by 'something more systematic'. But this is precisely what theoreticians want to do.

In the dialogue *Phaidros* Plato discusses rhetoric and medicine. Medicine, he says, deals with human beings. Physicians, therefore, must know what human beings are. Now physicians did have such information, but it was implicit and empirical. A large part of it was in the eyes and in the body and it was subjected to their faults and idiosyncrasies. For Plato, who regarded mathematics as a paradigm of knowledge and who, like many people after him thought mathematical reasoning to be completely transparent, such information had little to do with knowledge. Knowledge, according to Plato, consists of statements which are acquired and tested by following certain rules. *Not uncontrollable changes of the body but clear directives of the mind constitute knowledge and decide about truth and falsehood.* Or, to use modern terms: knowledge comes from theories, not from experience.

Now it is interesting to see to what extent this philosophy still rules the administration of knowledge. Modern science, of course, is not only theory; it is theory based on experiment. That radically distinguishes it from the Platonic ideal of science. Yet modern philosophers of science for a long time paid little attention to experimental procedures. The Vienna Circle divided statements into theoretical statements and observation statements. The main problem was how theoretical terms received their meaning. In the late 1950s many philosophers of science spoke of an 'upward seepage of meaning' – like the sap in a plant, meaning flows from the observational roots of knowledge upwards towards the theoretical terms. Arguing that observations taken by themselves have no meaning whatsoever, I suggested to invert the order: meaning flows from theories towards the observations. In both cases it was assumed that producing observational statements was a simple matter – clever experimentalists certainly would know how to obtain them.

Clever experimentalists did know how to obtain observation statements but in a way that overthrew the entire positivistic scheme. To start with, experimentalists rely on an enormous amount of tacit knowledge. They do not simply record what nature says, they drive their equipment like racing car drivers drive cars, often pushing it to the limit, and then make intuitive judgements about the reactions obtained (example: Baade on Mount Wilson in 1942).[3] Moreover, the reports issued by a team are frequently the result of delicate negotiations between its members – they are political documents embodying compromises and completed under considerable pressure. The experimental level forms an entire culture whose relation to theory is far from clear.

And yet engineering schools in the United States and in Great Britain decided, in the late sixties, to replace instruction in engineering practice by engineering theory. The result was that engineering projects started using a 'top-down approach' – theoreticians develop models which they send to the site in the expectation that the practitioners there will have no difficulty realizing them. But practice and theory cannot be glued together in this simple-minded way.

Do not be misguided by the fact that the theoreticians did consider a wide variety of evidence and that their theories, therefore, have empirical backing. The theories involve idealizations which means that the evidence is being selected and processed in a special way. This does not affect the predictions which are made under equally idealized circumstances. It *does* affect the reliability of products made from material that has retained its idiosyncrasies, such as the shore of a river, the ground under a high-rise or the wind-pattern in a narrowly defined region. To evaluate a project an engineer needs both theoretical and on-site experience and this means that he should have theoretical as well as practical schooling. A variety of disasters has convinced some administrators that the top-down approach is defective and that engineering practice is an important part of the education even of an engineering theoretician. Read Ferguson, *Engineering and the Mind's Eye*, MIT Press, for details.[4] (Needless to say, a theoretical medicine that is based on theory and laboratory reports entirely is equally inadequate.)

To sum up this part of the argument: the knowledge we claim to possess, the very general knowledge provided by modern physical theory included, is an intricate web of theoretical principles and practical, almost bodily abilities and it cannot be understood by looking at theories exclusively. Most popular accounts of science and many philosophical analyses are therefore chimeras, pure and simple. They are as distorted and misleading as a history of art which regards paintings as natural phenomena of a special kind without ever mentioning the individuals lingering in their neighbourhood when they first appear.

Now if this conclusion is correct then many activities which are regarded with respect and awe cease to make sense. Every 'systematic' philosophical treatise that considers only ideas and their mutual relations is an exercise in futility. Embedded in an ongoing enterprise, ideas play an important, though not easily comprehended, role. Treated by themselves they are like fossils that are studied as abstract shapes, without considering the processes from which they arose.

Let me give you an example to show how complex such processes can be.

Galileo's work was subjected to a variety of constraints, some complementing, others contradicting each other. To start with there were the constraints of his *profession*. Galileo began as a mathematician. Mathematics was then regarded as a subject capable of proof but incapable of dealing with reality. Reality was the business of philosophers, who on the whole adopted an Aristotelian approach. Galileo wanted to argue that reality was mathematical in nature. Now there were sciences that used mathematics but also dealt with real things. They were called *mixed sciences*; optics and astronomy were the main examples. The status of both was somewhat doubtful – which lowered Galileo's difficulties but did not entirely eliminate them.

Next we have to consider the constraints of *theology*. The Council of Trent reaffirmed the authority of the Church. The Church was now the sole authority in Biblical matters and in those parts of secular knowledge which, in its opinion, had Biblical implications. Some churchmen, Bellarmino for example, conceded that the interpretation of Bible passages might be changed in the light of scientific proof. There are many Bible passages that suggest a flat Earth. Yet the sphericity of the Earth was a commonplace already in the twelfth century. But the reinterpretation was to be done by theologians, not by scientists dabbling in theology. And even here the situation was not entirely unambiguous – the church was not a monolith. There were special interest groups, Jesuits, Franciscans, Dominicans who viewed the basic doctrine in different ways and had different attitudes towards a compromise.

Which brings me to the matter of *patronage*. Trying to get ahead, a scientist or for that matter, any public person in need of money and influence, needed a patron. Then as now, patronage had its own rather complicated rules which occasionally conflicted with the rules of science. There are scholars who suggest that Galileo got into trouble not so much because he acted against church doctrine, but because he violated the rules of patronage *vis-à-vis* a powerful patron of his, Pope Urban VIII.

I have not yet mentioned the rules of science. *Experience* played a large role, both among Aristotelians and their opponents. Did Galileo pay attention to experience? Not always and certainly not when he spoke of exceptionless and merciless laws. After all, exceptions were the rule of the day, in biology where they were called monsters, in astronomy where even Tycho appealed to god's power to explain the appearance of a new star and in human affairs where the devil was invoked to account for many strange physiological and psychological events (the *Malleus Maleficarum* published about two centuries earlier is a veritable textbook of mental aberrations). Aristotle had paid attention to these matters – that's why he said that natural is what happens always *or almost always*. St Thomas had opposed on the ground that God was stable. Ockham had pointed out that ascribing stability to God means restricting God's power. All we can do is to note what God has done and to try systematizing what we find: laws of nature are not in nature, they are mental constructs ordering events we basically do not and cannot understand. Descartes returned to stability – and so did Galileo, Ockham, experience and Aristotle notwithstanding. Already here it becomes clear that his procedure depended not so much on rules as on a choice between rules.

Among the rules, the *rules of argument* were most important. Three types of argument were distinguished: demonstration, dialectical arguments and rhetorical arguments. Demonstration started from well-established true premises and led to well-established true results. Aristotle explained the rules of demonstration in his *Analytics*. Demonstration was possible in mathematics and in certain parts of physics. A dialectical argument used common opinions, of scholars and of common sense and using them, tried to arrive at the truth. It went back and forth between different opinions until a single opinion remained – for the time being. Aristotle explained dialectical arguments in his *Topics*. Finally there were rhetorical arguments or PR, as we call such arguments today. Rhetorical arguments had the purpose to make opponents accept an opinion without regard to the truth or the falsehood of the opinion, though not without using these words. Here again Aristotle led the way, in his *Rhetoric*. Presenting certain ideas a writer therefore had a choice – he could choose demonstration, dialectic or rhetoric. Some authors claim that the amount of rhetoric increased during the debate over Copernicus, not only on the side of Galileo but on the side of his opponents as well, and that it has increased ever since.

Finally – in my presentation, but by no means as regards matters of fact – we have *Galileo's temper*. He was an easily irascible man, greedy for recognition, full of contempt for people not up to his standards.

Now imagine Galileo preparing his *Dialogue on the two Chief World Systems*. We do not know the relative weight these constraints assumed in his mind. However, they were there, he was aware of them, he was aware of the conflict between some of them and he had to make a choice. His choice was motivated by whatever tacit knowledge had accumulated in his mind, which in turn was modified by his character and, more specifically, by his mood of the moment. Many factors, not a single clear train of thought, shaped the final product. This is what happens when an intelligent and imaginative person, making use of past knowledge and trying to stay close to standards thought to be important, produces a theory, a work of art, an experiment, a movie or what have you.

And now that the product is before us, the systematizers can stretch it out on their rack, analyse it, and relate its ingredients to their favourite categories. In the philosophy of science the process has been called 'logical reconstruction', the idea being that the great inventors don't know what they are doing and need a reconstruction to tell them what they have achieved. The trouble with such an approach is that the reconstructed formulations are mostly barren – they don't have the power to suggest new actions, ideas, procedures. Only the incomprehensible utterances of scientists seem to have such power. Which means either that there cannot be any discoveries unless one leaves the house of reason, or that the house of reason is very different from what philosophers and other idea-mongers make it out to be. It is no use objecting that scientists (artists, politicians, etc.) are often inspired by philosophical ideas. If they are, then only because they are thoroughly transforming them. Philosophical ideas are a kind of food which they consume, digest, occasionally throw up again, but often change into material of an entirely different kind – into the unrecognizably beautiful body of a theory, an experiment, a new kind of medicine, a building or a symphony. Of course – the process is rare. Most people simply imitate words, ideas, established habits. They are not worse for that – except when they start believing that their way is the only way there is and the only way that should be financed and imposed on others.

Discussion

QUESTION: What was your aim in telling us your story of Greek philosophy?

FEYERABEND: My aim was to tell a story that would not be too boring and enlightening to some small extent. For example, it would reveal features which in modern science are concealed behind technicalities.

QUESTION: Of course when you choose a story rather than another it means that . . .

FEYERABEND: It is because it's more entertaining and also more complex. I know some people prefer what they call a systematic account. Such an account is about concepts, not about people and it shows how these concepts are related to each other. This is also a story but to me it seems to be a very unrealistic one. It is as if one described the life of a person by merely saying that she was born, then got into business and finally died, describing all these things as if they happened simultaneously. Also, why use the concepts that occur in the usual systematic accounts and not others? And is it realistic to assume that concepts are ever as precise as a systematic account requires? You try to nail them down – though why you should do that you do not say. And having nailed them down in your book you think they will be nailed down in your mind and that others will understand them as you do. A very naive assumption! A story tells you how certain concepts arose, why they became important, why they changed and, above all, why they became a public malaise. It also informs you – and I have tried to do that in my third lecture, I believe – that absolutely precise concepts would stop thought and that conceptual development presupposes ambiguity; not a well-defined ambiguity that can be defined by another systematic account, but an ambiguity that shows itself in the course of a person's life. So, it is a *subjective* matter and you have to tell the story of the person. For all these reasons I think that a systematic account, far from making things clear, replaces the real world of thought and action by a chimera. Believing what you read in a book on epistemology is like believing that the action on the stage of a theatre is all there is and that there are no people behind the scenes turning on the lights, changing colours, putting items where they are supposed to be, a jug, for example, or a telephone, ringing the telephone and bringing down the curtain.

QUESTION: When a scientist applies for research funds he can't just say that he is going to tell a nice story . . .

FEYERABEND: Well, to start with, many scientists lie – not in a direct, shameless way, for that they are too full of good intentions, but in an indirect manner that is not even clear to themselves. Secondly, they will of course tell a story. They will tell what they did, what their first results were, why they were dissatisfied with them and so on. The final story that enters the annals of science will be severely streamlined. It will be about facts and theories. But that is a matter of style and tradition. Poets also produce severely streamlined products. There exist even views that assume that the products arose in that manner – the perfect poem suddenly shone forth in the poet's mind. These views are not correct – just ask any poet. Why are they here? Well, to explain that, you have to tell a story. Behind the streamlining of scientific results lies the assumption that they describe reality as it is independently of the actions of scientists. The assumption that there is such a reality is highly questionable – so the question arises again: Why do people believe it? And giving the official reasons does not answer your question for you can still ask why the reasons sound compelling to them. Why do they accept them? So we have to go into history and, with that, storytelling.

QUESTION: What is truth for you?

FEYERABEND: Well, sometimes it is one thing, sometimes another. Do you really believe that there is a brief explanation that would satisfy you and contain all the ways in which I use the term 'true'? Or, more generally, that there is something which can explain why people say that the Big Bang is true, the existence of God is true, the suffering of Christ is true, the wickedness of my mother-in-law is true and that it is true that right now I am hungry? Do you assume that we mean the same thing in all these cases and that this thing can be explained in a sentence or two? Before a judge a witness is supposed to speak the truth, the truth and nothing but the truth. Compare with this The Truth of Christianity. The first is about details, the second about the entire history of humanity. Of course, it's the same word but this doesn't mean there is the same sense behind it, or any sense at all.

QUESTION: You have said that some scientists lie . . .

FEYERABEND: Some occasionally, some often, some never.

QUESTION: My question is: What should they do? What should they write in their applications for research funds?

FEYERABEND: I am not saying they should not lie. Very often I would say one should lie. If telling the truth hurts a person, then I would certainly lie, unless it caused some other damage. I have no principle such as 'always speak the truth'. To me such a principle seems utterly ridiculous.

A young lady once wrote to Kant. She had a big problem and she asked him if one could lie to a person under certain circumstances, namely, when knowing the truth would hurt that person very much. Immanuel Kant wrote back that one must tell the truth under all circumstances because to tell a lie means violating the whole of humanity. The way we talk to each other constitutes a bond and this bond is based on truthfulness. Well, first of all if this lady told a lie, let's say, to her mother, just to make her life easier, she would not have hurt anybody in Somalia. The idea that what you say to one person affects all of humanity is a philosophical nightmare, a product of a philosophical Doctor Mabuse, who tries to direct the affairs of humans, invisibly, from his dusty office.

There are more complicated cases involving the question of truth. For example, many people believe, and perhaps rightly so, that what they perceive with their senses does not correspond to how things are. It's the same in personal matters, when you come to know somebody and he smiles at you, he is friendly and so on – and then you have a suspicion and you wonder if the guy is sincere: What does he really think about me, what is the truth about the matter? The guy himself may wonder if his first positive impression of me corresponds to 'what I really am'. Not that this is a very clear idea – maybe I am not one thing but many – but it does make some vague sense. So occasionally, when things are very undecided, looking for the truth means assuming that the world is built in a certain way, that there is a performance and a machinery behind the performance and that knowing the machinery you will understand a little better what the performance is all about. In such a case – and I think that the case of science is like that – speaking of truth means making an assumption about the way the world is built and acting on it. There is a book that made a great impression upon me. It was written some time ago by Tom Wolfe, an American journalist, and its title is *The Bonfire of the Vanities*.[5] It's a funny story. It starts with the description of a simple event. After some time, many different groups of people become interested in what happened, and they become interested for all sorts of reasons: political reasons, religious reasons and personal reasons. Different institutions start their process of discovering the truth, each one of them with its own methods, prejudices, each one of them trying to further its own interest. In the end the event disappears and it is clear that, except for the participants, nobody will ever know what really happened. Even the participants gradually forget, things start looking different to them. Well, in such a case it makes good sense to say: so-and-so happened, that is the truth. We could have found out – but we won't, not the way things are set up. But, you see, it takes a long story to explain what happened in this case and what truth means here. No definition can replace the story because other cases need not be like this one.

Take the old idea that the Earth is at rest in the centre of the universe. Many people believed that and the most outstanding minds of the time had strong arguments to support the belief. Today we believe that the Earth moves, so it is hard for us to understand why the old belief could ever have gained acceptance. We are liable to think along the following lines: the Earth moves. Quite definitely it does. These guys said it is at rest. They certainly missed something either because of their prejudices, or because they did not think clearly enough. And the assumption is that there is the same reality in both cases, and some people see it clearly while others are misled by all sorts of obstacles. But the older thinkers assumed that real is what can be directly observed – what seamlessly joins common sense, and the 'modern' thinkers assume that 'reality' is hidden and that our senses are incapable of grasping it directly. The senses deceive, not only now and then, but always: the Parmenidean position. Now there are things that directly join common sense and form an entire world and there are things that are recondite and have to be found by instruments and speculation. They, too, form an entire world. Neither of the two worlds is perfect and without problems – but they do form two different sets to which to refer and the transition from one to the other cannot be described as a transition from error to truth – that is the point of view of the second world. So, again, talking of truth makes certain assumptions about the world – and these need not be accepted.

QUESTION: I have an increasing feeling that there is a misunderstanding between this audience and Paul. I had the same feeling when I read local newspapers reporting on this conference. Even some specialists' comments maybe missed the point about Paul's real concern. Many people seem to think that Paul is an epistemologist and my opinion is that Paul doesn't deserve this insult. This is not his concern.

In our century epistemology has been identified with essentially two approaches. The first one deals with the origin and the real ground of knowledge, it includes empiricism and other schools which investigate whether knowledge is based on experience or on reason, on induction or deduction and so on. According to the second approach, which is more in the Popperian style, the task of the philosophy of science is just to give, to impose, a method. I figure that Paul's real concern is none of these things. Maybe he isn't completely against these two approaches, but this isn't his own job anyway. I think that in these past four days he showed us that his concern is to investigate the strange link existing between theoretical knowledge, theoretical reason and empirical, concrete knowledge. I don't think that his task is just to show us what the real ground of knowledge is or what the right methods to attain scientific knowledge are.

My job essentially consists in a reflection about social sciences and human sciences and I find Paul's investigation of the strange link existing between concrete, practical knowledge and theories or meta-theories very problematic in the social sciences, and I am very glad that the same problem arises in the hard sciences too. We are often shocked when we analyse, for example, the practice of a clinical psychologist, of a psychiatrist or of a politician because there is always a kind of widespread illusion that, if a politician or a clinician obtains some good effects, it is because his theory was right, was true. But then a detailed analysis makes you realize that there is no link between the two things and that they really overlap.

For example, are we sure that in 1918 Lenin won the revolution because he had the right theory about a revolution? Of course he was a philosopher, a very important Marxist philosopher, but today's historical reconstructions provide us with more details: maybe Lenin won by chance or by a kind of grace.

I think Paul's real teaching is to warn us not to take for granted that there is a deduction from a theory, from a vision of the world, to scientific practice. Maybe you don't have a method which is useful for everybody, but you shouldn't believe that you are successful because you follow a good theory, but because of your art. I wonder if Paul agrees with my reconstruction of his real concern.

FEYERABEND: Well, since you pose the problem in this way, I would say the following. In many domains (not only in the domain of knowledge), there are practical efforts and on the other side there are people who try to give a general account of the whole domain. For example, take the domain of law. For a long time people judged crimes according to a common law which consisted of traditional ways of dealing with a great variety of 'crimes'. Common law historically developed case by case, until finally there were many kinds of different prescriptions which one could memorize, or collect in a list. Examples of common laws can be found already in Homer. Achilles' shield which contains a presentation of the whole universe has also a law court – twelve elderly men sitting in judgement. The cases are brought before them and are explained to them. The twelve men have lived for a long time; they remember a great variety of cases, they remember how people dealt with them and they judge the new case accordingly – from their memory and their perception of similarities and differences. This is case law or common law.

But there were always people who were not satisfied with mere lists and who tried to tie the lists together with, or even to replace them by, more general and universally valid laws – laws that did not vary from case to case and according to the memories and the intuitions of some old men. It is easy to see that such general laws will be more tyrannical and less adapted to the situations of different people than case laws.

In other areas the situation is exactly the same. Take the theatre. Here we have theatrical practice – Aeschylus, Euripides, Sophocles, for example, and we have Aristotle, who gave a general definition of tragedy. Aristotle's definition is interesting but it does not fit Greek practice and it is much poorer than this practice. For example, following Aristotle you cannot have discussions such as those between Apollo, Orest and the Furies in the third part of the *Oresteia*.

In painting, for a long time and up to the fifteenth century, painters were brought up in schools. There the pupils first learned how to prepare wooden panels or the ground for a fresco, they learned how to mix colours, varnishes, glazes, they learned simple drawings and they learned how to fill in the sketches prepared by the masters. All this is explained in Cennino Cennini's book.[6] And then suddenly, somebody discovered perspective! Perspective gives a general account of the structure of pictures and one of its first texts was written by Leon Battista Alberti. Alberti defines a painting as the cross-section of the rays which come from the object to the eyes; so there's this bundle of rays, there's the object, there's the eye and in between, their cross-section.[7] It is a purely mathematical definition. In order to paint, the painter now has to know mathematics and geometry and the physical effect of colours and so on. This new definition turned painters from practitioners into theoreticians. Many painters got fascinated by this new play-thing, perspective, and they started studying it. Uccello neglected his wife, his children, because he was captured by this wonderful thing, perspective. But the painters, da Vinci and Raphael among them, soon found out that a painting does not work as the theory of perspective says it does. So the theory had to be modified by exceptions here and there and a new practice arose just as there is now a practice of engineering side by side with abstract physical theory.

Using examples such as these I would say that there are people who think in abstract terms and people who think and act from their imagination and their memory of concrete situations. In addition there is an interesting interaction between the two domains. Practical people may get interested in theories and improve, or ruin their practice as a result. Theoreticians trying to apply their abstract ideas to experience, practice and common sense may modify them here and there. Theoreticians in addition often claim to possess true knowledge, while the practitioners have only the shadow of it. Therefore theoreticians often are more respected than the dirty workers, etc. I already talked about the different attitudes people have towards theoreticians and experimentalists and the historical background of the difference. Now what interests me is the interaction between the two domains – how it develops over time, in a certain region or society; what it does to people, their lives and their reputations. I am on the side of practice because it seems to be more democratic, but I realize that theory can improve practice, only, this is a complicated matter and not easily understood. That's another thing that interests me.

In the case of the sciences, there are people who say that science obeys abstract rules and owes its success to them. Others, Einstein among them, say that scientists use what best fits a certain situation. I am inclined to side with Einstein. And indeed, a scientist is an explorer of the unknown. An explorer heeds instruments, vehicles and clothing – will he use the same instruments, vehicles and clothing in Uganda and on the South Pole? Certainly not. But nature's differences are much larger than the differences between Uganda and the South Pole. To judge theories a researcher needs abstract measuring instruments – methodological rules. Is it to be assumed that the same rules will be capable of judging all cases? That would be a very unrealistic assumption to make. You measure the temperature of a room by using a thermometer and the temperature of solar radiation by using a bolometer. Both are rather useless in ironworks – and so on. This means you have to adapt your methods to the case you are dealing with and have to invent new methods when new cases come along. This is what Einstein says – and here he is on the side of the practical people. Popper with his principle of falsification is on the side of the theoreticians: science is defined by its method and the method is falsification. But the number of scientists who collapse in front of a single big falsification is rather small and science would look very different if it were run by them exclusively. So, whatever general rules there are, they fail if taken as a summary of scientific practice though they may work in particular scientific achievements. The best way is to take them as rules of thumb.

So, I would not frown upon the abstract approach, I would only deny that the abstract approach gives you the essence of a field, as if people engaged in a concrete approach were stumbling around like blind men and women and only by chance they get the right result, while the abstract approach tells you what is really going on. Just remember what I said about engineering and the example of agriculture in my second lecture when commenting on the abstract approach recommended by Monod.

Dehumanizing Humans

To take another example, consider drama. The Aristotelian theory of tragedy is ingenious and rather simple. Read the *Poetics* if you have the chance: it is a small book. The theory expressed in it does not fit Greek tragedy, but it had great influence. It led to the writing of great tragedies in the late Middle Ages, in France . . . of course, great from the point of view of those who are attracted by this kind of stuff. It also led to reactions that furthered the cause of drama. And it invites us today to use new approaches in sociology. For Aristotle the important thing in tragedy is that it reveals the underlying laws of society; therefore, he says, tragedy is more philosophical than history. And it is certainly a better way of comprehending these laws than a sociological essay full of footnotes and technical terms. At any rate, it is not true that philosophers and scientists and other people using Big Words are closer to reality than others, and that they can show us the way while we can't show them anything. They can show us interesting things alright, but so can magicians, acupuncturists, birdwatchers, cooks, engineers and guys from the neighbourhood who just discovered that they have healing powers (my former TV repairman in Meilen is an example). The fact that there are such people should be taught in schools and the children should learn how to look for them. Of course, science is important, both because of the positive contributions it has to make and because of the fact that its droppings are to be found everywhere: it needs a scientist to clean what a scientist has messed up! What is troubling – and what will always remain troubling to me – is that such people have a special position in society. They had it when myths played a major role, they have it now. But perhaps I am worrying unduly. People like to have heroes they can look up to. And, naturally, they will give them a special position.

Incidentally, let me talk a little about the role of practice in the sciences. I already told you, I think in the third lecture, that science is not all theory; there are also experiments and those who design, control and perform large-scale experiments look at matters in a way that differs considerably from the way of the theoreticians, or at least so it seems. To start with, they use 'approximations'. These are not just sloppy theories, but intellectual instruments of a special kind. They are adapted to things one can see and touch and function as a kind of common-sense discourse. Then they use experimental equipment; this is like driving a car. You learn acting with the equipment and then you use it relying on your reactions, not on statements you have memorized. When Los Angeles was under total blackout in 1943, because of the scare about the Japanese, Walter Baade made a series of observations with the big telescope on Mount Palomar. He was an excellent observer who knew all the tricks the telescope could play on him and who had a lot of tricks in return. He knew also how to push the telescope to the limit – just as a racing car driver knows what his car can take, and that it can take a little more, and a little more. It is almost as if the telescope or the car had become part of one's own body. This 'tacit knowledge' as Michael Polanyi called it plays a large role in the experimental parts of science and it needs the immediate reactions of a person, not just 'objective' statements, to become effective.

Now the interesting thing is that the same happens in the realm of theory. No theory springs forth from the head of the theoretician like Athena sprang from the forehead of Zeus. There are vague anticipations, truncated parts of what might be a theory, they are adapted to the boundary conditions the theoretician regards as important which may be the ways in which things are formulated in his favourite mathematical discipline (algebra, topology, etc.), or some experimental results. This preparatory activity also makes use of 'tacit knowledge' i.e. of guesses as to how a pseudo-theory might act in extreme cases and how its consequences might change when it is transformed in a certain way. The final product, the published theory, looks of course static. No wonder; it is printed on paper which changes very little over the years. But changes precede it, changes follow it and they are all changes tied to the intuitive knowledge the theoretician has accumulated over the years – which again means tacit knowledge. Thus it seems that the opposition between theory and experiment is not an opposition between theory – understood as Platonic ideas – and a moving and partly subjective practice; it is an opposition between two kinds of (moving and subjective) practice, the one applied to things, the other to formulae. Platonism, however, is a dream hovering above the two and doing justice to neither.

Let me add something else, because, you see, things are never simple. You talk a lot and arrive at A. Then you talk some more and non-A seems to become plausible. Then you talk still more and it seems that neither A nor non-A make sense – and so on. At any rate, the fact that it is not a good thing to present a theory as if it were Truth Herself should not prevent people from sticking to a theory they love, even if all the indicators they ask speak against the theory. I already told you that theories or world views may have a difficult birth and may bear fruit only centuries later. Examples are the atomic theory, the idea that the world has a beginning, the idea that the Earth moves, the idea that organisms develop by a kind of adaptation – and so on. It pays to have faith and to be patient. I just mentioned an astronomer, Walter Baade. When he made the observations I described, the idea that the world has a beginning was being considered by astronomers, but was in great trouble. Some scientists did not like it because it reminded them of Christianity. Others pointed to the evidence: the age of the universe as calculated from Hubble's constant was smaller than the age of the Earth as calculated from terrestrial observations. Baade found that the Cepheids that had been used for calculating distances came in two kinds which differed in their relation between period and absolute luminosity, and that astronomers had used the wrong kind. That removed the blemish – but many astronomers had been willing to stay with the theory despite it. Is this not a very irrational attitude? Not at all. The difficulties of a theory are due to a clash between two entities – the theory, and the means used to criticize it. They show that there is a clash, they do not say where the fault lies. Those who regard the theory as refuted trust the means of criticism – the evidence, the arguments that build on it. Those who retain the theory conjecture that the means of criticism are faulty though they cannot say exactly where the fault lies. It is the same as trusting a friend or a client in the face of damaging reports, and trying to clear his or her name. It may take weeks, it may take years, it may never happen – and yet the accused party may be entirely innocent. So, it is not irrational to stick to a losing cause, though many people who believe the world to be rather transparent may say it is. But then accepting an apparently successful view as a guide, in research, politics, medicine, for judging people and things, is like electing an apparently good guy for public office in the hope he will succeed. It means that we shall support the view and listen to its advice for the time being.

This has important consequences for education. Children in school are never told that the president of their country will remain in office forever. No. They are told that he was elected, why he was elected and that the next election is only four years away. They will also be told that he may be impeached – that he might be out of office a few months from now. Yet, when it comes to physics they are told that everything consists of elementary particles, not for the time being, not until impeachment, but absolutely. They are not told that other candidates are waiting in the wings, that they may be discouraged because a current view has been in power for such a long time, but that they are there nevertheless. Nor are they told that the current view may soon be voted out of office and how this will happen. The general public is equally misguided; for example they are expected to pay taxes for enterprises that may collapse in a matter of years. I do not say that they should not pay; I say that they should be informed of the nature of the risk involved. Not many people would be ready to pay money for Clinton in 2001. And this is why all this talk about truth is severely misleading. It is true that Clinton is president (I hope you are reading this when this statement is still true) – and everybody knows what it means. It is also true that information flows from DNA to its surroundings, never the other way around. I would say it is true in the same sense in which it is true that Clinton is President – a few years from now it won't be true anymore. And I would also say that this is what ought to be taught in school. But what happens there is that a good procedure – that you may stay with a view of ill-repute forever – is turned into its opposite by asserting that it has been found true and will forever remain the foundation of our knowledge.

QUESTION: I would like to illustrate a concrete case, which is important for the social sciences: the theory of von Neumann-Morgenstern, decision theory in a situation of uncertainty. This theory is based on an axiomatic structure, with a set of axioms and rules (of consistency, transitivity, and so on). From the axioms a function of utility is derived, which takes into account such uncertainties. The theory says that people making their decisions, behave in such a way that the function of utility is maximized, under certain assumptions and circumstances. This theory clashes with practical results, there are many violations and problems. My question then is: What should we do with such a theory that on one side seems very interesting and important and on the other side clashes with facts? We have four options: 1. look for a different theory; 2. refine the function of utility; 3. modify the set of axioms of the theory; 4. consider the theory as valid only under particular circumstances. What should we do when such a variety of possible options is in front of us?

FEYERABEND: My suggestion to proliferate and to make use of many different points of view, theories, methodologies is not directed at scientists. Scientists have their own ways of doing things. In some of my earlier writings, I wanted to interfere in their activity and I said: you won't make discoveries unless you proliferate. Now I would say that the only interference that counts is interference by the people on the spot. Why? Because they know the details including the details that are not written down but reside in their experience. So, in your case I would say: do what you think is best.

It is different when we are talking about general education. Here the students should be informed about everything that is going on in their society and in the world and not only about the leading fashions. They should know that there are alternatives, that they are unpopular, that one cannot earn much money by defending them, that they have some advantages – and so on. Now, for the particular group of scientists who face the problems you have described, I would say that I would have to be part of this research-group before I open my mouth. It would be presumptuous of me to make suggestions from the outside. Somebody in this group may propose to stick to a certain approach in spite of its difficulties and of its apparent uselessness because (s)he believes that some result may be obtained by means of some slight modifications. (S)he may assemble followers. And who knows what may happen when many people start working on that approach? Of course, who knows what may happen if you do the opposite thing? There are scientists who ask their fellow experts to help them – for example, they may ask a methodologist or a philosopher of science. That is OK, for in this case we have a scientist to filter whatever is being proposed through his experience. But it would be a mistake for any scientist to follow a methodologist just because he is presumed to be an expert, without any input from his part.

QUESTION: This amounts to shifting the problem to the bad education of those who participate in a research group: how can we improve matters then?

FEYERABEND: Yes, the problem is that of a very bad education. I think that if the general educational background were a little more varied, maybe people would know a little more about other fields and would not be so one-sided. And by that I don't mean that they add the slogans of another discipline to those of their own. I mean that they arrive at a kind of synthesis. Take philosophy. I am in favour of scientists being more philosophical – that they don't take their own rules so terribly seriously, but show some kind of perspective. Many scientists are doing that already, but there is still a large bunch that regards certain achievements as if they were divine inspiration. What has been achieved in philosophy should become part of the tacit knowledge of the sciences, not an item that is added from the outside.

QUESTION: My discipline is literature and, even if you have somehow said that you do not want to have anything to do with deconstruction, I think you meant with Derrida's ideas. I felt your reading of the history of philosophy very close at least to the so-called 'critical theory', which is a kind of deconstruction with a particular stress on history, on historicism. What is your position *vis-à-vis* other contemporary philosophers which we, men of letters, find so useful?

My second question deals with the possibility of exposing the basis, the origin of philosophy, in terms of a tension between two poles: the masculine and the feminine.

FEYERABEND: About the concentration on texts: I told a story and it was based on texts: unfortunately that is all there is. Greek tragedy, however, was not merely a text. It was movement, sound, there were visual impressions – I told you how according to reports people shrank back when the Furies entered the stage, instruments were involved and so on. Anybody who reads the tragedies has to be aware that what he got is only a small part and perhaps not even the most important part of a much more comprehensive entity. A multimedia presentation like that cannot be reduced to and then analysed from the perspective of, a text. Same about poetry. I told you that ancient poetry, Xenophanes for example, but also less intellectualized poetry, was recited, often as instruments. Philosophical texts were published by being read aloud to a selected audience and they were not always regarded as decisive. A text, said Plato, is a poor substitute for what really counts, which is the living exchange between different people. Interestingly enough the same is true of part of the modern knowledge process. Advances in mathematics occur in seminars, at conferences. The printed reports are far behind in substance and depth. Remember what I said about the thesis that science is a system of statements, i.e. a grandiose text. It is an absurd caricature of what science is. As far as I am concerned this whole concern about texts is the result of a degeneration of multimedia events or of life. There is one idea I understand about deconstruction and it is that you cannot nail down ideas by writing. I heartily agree. I would even say that you cannot nail them down by any means. Another idea is that there is no real distinction between literature and philosophy except that the one is livelier than the other. I again agree, though I know a lot of boring poems.

Philosophy arising from a tension between male and female? It is an interesting thought which has some support in Aeschylus: the new law, which is not a philosophical law but is more general, is a male law, it is the law of Zeus and Apollo and the old law was feminine. There is a tension between the two and Aischylos explores it in a masterful manner. He also wants both laws to guide the city, not only one of them. Most philosophers reacted to common sense and tradition. I would say that most early philosophers were crudely, very crudely masculine – simple principles, neglect, even hatred of subjectivity. Part of their objections was directed at Homer – but the epics are not simply feminine. In Hesiod the basic principles have a twofold aspect – they are partly personal, partly abstract. This is a very complex situation and I don't know what to make of it.

QUESTION: I would like you to explain the sub-title of your book *Against Method*. You wrote it is an 'anarchist', and moreover from a 'dadaist' point of view.

FEYERABEND: The whole thing is a joke. Look, it says 'outline of an anarchist theory of knowledge'. Now, what is anarchism? Disorder. What is theory? Order. Combining both is a Dadaist trick addressed to those anarchists who want to be anarchists and have a theory, too – an impossible undertaking. An Italian anarchist once wrote me and asked me to contribute to a selection of utterances about anarchism. I replied in a somewhat mocking letter. Well, he printed the stuff – but reduced to a paragraph of serious cerebration. Well, if this is what an anarchist does, then bye-bye anarchism! And there is a second reason why I used the subtitle and it is this: I am convinced that a philosopher of science who believes in the laws of reason, and is confronted with the history of science in all its splendour, would be so shocked that he would say that science is pure anarchy.

QUESTION: I know that there was a very long discussion between you and your opponents about your famous sentence 'anything goes' (*tutto fa brodo*). Very often you denounced a kind of misunderstanding, pointing out that this was not your real point of view, but that it was a logical conclusion from the theoretical point of view. I think that also in Italy you are well known as the man who believes that 'anything goes', so you may like to spend some words on this.

FEYERABEND: *Tutto fa brodo*: it is true! The most surprising things lead to great discoveries! Those who think that new things can be found only by wandering along a precisely defined path are wrong. You cannot foresee what kind of silly move will lead you to a new insight or to a new discovery. The move is 'silly' only when compared with the general opinion of the time in which you live. For example, we assume we are standing on solid earth. This is our first and most basic experience. Anaximander says that the Earth floats in mid-air. It is a shock, just think of it: nothing floats in mid-air, I mean, if you put something up there, it will fall down. Yet, Anaximander says that the entire heavy Earth floats in mid-air. Was this anarchy, when measured by modern standards? It certainly was. But it developed and something came out of it. So, 'anything goes' means only 'don't restrict your imagination' because a very silly idea can lead to a very solid result. Also, don't restrict your imagination by logic. Many fruitful theories, if examined with the magnifying glass of the logicians, are internally inconsistent. But scientists have the talent of moving around the trouble-spots and to get ahead despite of them. Besides, an inconsistency is deadly only if you have rigid concepts. But concepts are like putty – they can be shaped in many different ways. In sum, I would say that indeed 'anything goes'.

QUESTION: I got the impression that you have used the word 'theory' in many different senses. In physics this word is used in a well-defined sense. So when you talk of 'theory of tragedy' or 'of painting', do you agree that it is rather a matter of definition of tragedy or of painting?

FEYERABEND: I agree completely. I used the word 'theory' intentionally but perhaps unfortunately in a very sloppy way, meaning by it any kind of general account. I left aside all further subdivisions. In Euclid we have postulates, definitions and axioms. Different editions distribute these terms in a different way – what is an axiom in one may become a postulate in another. What interests me is how people deal with generalities. Some formulate theories, i.e. statements which are general in intention, some formulate rules which can have exceptions, some are content with expectations. There was a long discussion within the philosophy of science on the distinction between theories and laws. For example, people would speak of Newton's 'theory' of gravitation, but of Kepler's 'laws', and then try to define a distinction between them. Well, one distinction is that Kepler's laws apply to the planets only while Newton's theory is supposed to apply to everything. But, then you speak of the second law of thermodynamics and this is supposed to be generally valid. So, I would say, you better remain vague.

QUESTION: Maybe there is a third way of dealing with that, replacing the word 'theory' with 'rule' as in Wittgenstein's terms, like the rule of a game. Don't you agree with this?

Dehumanizing Humans

FEYERABEND: No, I don't think that helps at all. It implies a certain view of regularities I don't find particularly attractive – but that is a long story.

QUESTION: In relation to what you said the first day, talking about the Furies, namely that the mother was seen as just a breeding oven, I would like to understand the reasons why in such an evolved society as it was in ancient Greece, women were not considered as such, as women.

FEYERABEND: In the play itself this idea is introduced by Apollo, who represents a new kind of religion. For the Furies the mother is not just a breeding oven, it is a blood relative. So there are two parties and the question is how the new party arose. I do not know that. Athena's solution is that both parties have made contributions to the history of the city and should be remembered by it. Was it implausible to make the assumption that women are a breeding oven? Not on the basis of what was known at the time. Women gave birth. They bore the child for nine months. They became pregnant as a result of intercourse. That was known and that is not being denied. What is being denied is, to use modern terms, that women make a genetic contribution. That is a very subtle matter which at that time could be only dealt with by ideology.

QUESTION: I would like to know how strongly you hold the distinction between practical and theoretical knowledge, since I think there are many kinds of arguments against this distinction. For example, the professions, as they were in antiquity, in the Middle Ages up to the nineteenth century, had a non-written way to convey knowledges, a way different from the one used by theoreticians, but knowledges were conveyed anyway. And the university has the task to train young people, and this is an extremely practical task. Moreover, with regard to definitions, to the fact that some people are specialists in words, in giving definitions: this is a practical activity of the so-called theoreticians.

FEYERABEND: I myself would not take the distinction too seriously but it was taken seriously at various periods in history and it was used by putting those classified as practical on a lower level – and that was what I wanted to talk about. I told you about Plato's distinction between habit and true knowledge, about the way in which some philosophers separated physical theory from experiment and ascribed a secondary role to the latter and so on, and I also told you that to my mind even high-grade mathematics is practical as long as it is being developed. Now, when the Universities started in Europe in the tenth century, there were two groups of subjects, the *trivium* and the *quadrivium*. The *trivium* was grammar, rhetoric, dialectic; the *quadrivium* was arithmetic, geometry, music and then sometimes astronomy, sometimes something else. Painting and architecture for a long time were not university subjects. Why? Because they did not have a theoretical part with abstract principles and precise rules. So when perspective was discovered, the defenders of artisans who looked a little further said: 'Now these people have a chance of having their subject taught at the universities – so let us write a few books about the matter.' – and they wrote the books and they succeeded. So this is a distinction which lasted for a long time and had great practical effects despite the fact it was rather unrealistic.

QUESTION: I don't deny that the distinction between theoretical and practical knowledge was made. I want to stress the fact that if the so-called theoreticians build up a theory of theoretical knowledge, this is simply to specify themselves as a group, as a profession, they just have to qualify themselves.

FEYERABEND: Perfectly correct. It is group identity and power play.

QUESTION: Wittgenstein said that not all knowledge is explicitly applicable. Nevertheless, in the field of artificial intelligence many people are trying to make many common activities explicit, and they meet with many obstacles: It is very difficult to interpret such behaviour procedures from an explicit, theoretical point of view. It is very difficult to give rules for it. This shifts the distinction theoretical-practical to a different level: we might talk of a distinction between theories acquired by doing and theories acquired by observing. For example, we could draw a distinction between a guy who follows principles of doing and a guy who follows how other people behave, so that if everybody crosses the road with red, he crosses with red too. Now, my question is: Do you think that there is a nucleus of knowledge which is not transmissible, what you called a tacit knowledge?

FEYERABEND: The position of those who believe in tacit knowledge is not that tacit knowledge cannot be transmitted, but that it cannot be transmitted by means of a written text. Tacit knowledge can be transmitted by instruction, like instruction for boxing, piano-playing: all this stuff is transmissible, but not by reading a book.

QUESTION: In everyday life it happens very often that one makes use of technology without knowing anything about what is beyond it. Science produces effects upon normal life by means of things whose workings people normally do not understand, although they can deal with them.

FEYERABEND: Yes, it is what happens with a television set: you can turn it on, turn it off, find the right channel, but you do not know what goes on inside. It was not always so. Some time ago many people could repair their cars and their radios. Today they not only lack the knowledge, they also lack the necessary equipment. Cars and radios do not have many exchangeable parts, so you must either buy a big and expensive ingredient, or you throw away the whole things. Technology now encourages ignorance. So I would agree.

Editor's Notes

INTRODUCTION

1   These lectures took place from the 4th to the 8th of May 1992 at the University of Trent, Italy. The videotapes were transcribed, and then edited by Feyerabend in July 1993. The working title was 'Conflict and Harmony'. Chapter titles, notes and references were added by the editor. Minor adjustments were made to the typescript.

2   Feyerabend began the lecture series with a brief apology, explaining that he usually develops these ideas over the course of a semester, allowing him to get to know his audience more personally and to adapt his ideas accordingly.

3   The only book that Feyerabend finished thereafter was his autobiography, *Killing Time* (1995), which was written on his death-bed. At the time, he was also working on *Conquest of Abundance* (1999), which was never completed. A third volume of collected papers, *Knowledge, Science and Relativism*, appeared posthumously (1999). More recently, the publication of *Naturphilosophie* (2009), which was written from 1974 to 1976 as a companion to *Against Method* (1975) was well received in the German-speaking world. An English translation is forthcoming.

4   See John Preston's 'Paul Feyerabend' in the *Stanford Encyclopedia of Philosophy*, and Feyerabend's *Killing Time* (1995), p. 68.

5   See Feyerabend's *Zur Theorie der Basissätze* (1951) Universitätsbibliothek, Wien.

6   Later he completely reversed his position, see and compare Feyerabend's 'Niels Bohr's Interpretation of the Quantum Theory' (1961) with 'On a Recent Critique of Complementarity: Part I' (1968) and 'On a Recent Critique of Complementarity: Part II' (1969a).

7   See Feyerabend's 'Review of *Philosophical Investigations*. By Ludwig Wittgenstein' (1955).

8   Feyerabend correspondence with Popper is currently being edited for publication.

9   See Kuhn (1962/1970). Feyerabend and Kuhn were colleagues at Berkeley in 1960. They arrived at the idea of incommensurability independently, but drew support from each other in developing it.

10   See Hoyningen-Huene (1995) and (2006).

11   See *Against Method* (1975, 1983, 1993, 2010).

12   See T. Theocharis and M. Psimopoulos 'Where Science has Gone Wrong' (1987). The label stuck, becoming the basis of a collection of papers on Feyerabend entitled *The Worst Enemy of Science? Essays on the Philosophy of Paul Feyerabend* (Munévar and Lamb 2000).

13   For example, as widely reported in the international press (15 January 2008), Pope Benedict XVI cancelled a visit to *La Sapienza*, a prestigious university in Rome, because lecturers and students protested against his views on Galileo. Faculty members at *La Sapienza* had reportedly signed a letter addressed to the university's rector, saying that Pope Benedict's views on Galileo 'offend and humiliate' them. The well-circulated letter explained that 'in the name of the secular nature of science we hope this incongruous event can be cancelled.' After the Pope's cancellation, the planned remarks were published, and Vatican Radio alleged that the protests at *La Sapienza* had 'a censorious tone'. The controversy was sparked by remarks made by Cardinal Ratzinger in 'The Crisis of Faith in Science', Parma, 15 March 1990, when he defended the Church's position on Galileo. Drawing on scientists and other experts, Cardinal Ratzinger specifically cited Feyerabend, who argued that the Church's treatment of Galileo had been 'rational and just'; see Feyerabend's 'Galileo – The Tyranny of Truth' (1985). On the basis of such expert opinions, Cardinal

Ratzinger concluded that 'It would be absurd . . . to construct a hurried apologetics' concerning Galileo's treatment.

14 See Feyerabend's *Farewell to Reason* (1987).

15 For more on the impact of the student revolutions in the late 1960s, see Preston's 'Paul Feyerabend' in *Stanford Encyclopaedia of Philosophy* (2009). For Feyerabend as a post-modernist philosopher, see for example, Preston's 'Science as Supermarket: 'Post-Modern' Themes in Paul Feyerabend's Later Philosophy of Science' (1998).

16 In his attempt to learn something positive from every tradition, Feyerabend's interests included subjects often dismissed in academic circles, such as astrology, witchcraft, voodoo and alternative medicine. See also Feyerabend's 'From Incompetent Professionalism to Professionalized Incompetence – The Rise of a New Breed of Intellectuals' (1978).

17 See for example Feyerabend's *Against Method* (1975), p. 46 and (1993), pp. 31–2 and p. 34. n. 2. Compare Feyerabend's 'Against Method: Outline of an Anarchistic Theory of Knowledge' (1970) and 'How to Be a Good Empiricist: A Plea for Tolerance in Matters Epistemological' (1963).

18 See Feyerabend's 'Ethics as a Measure of Scientific Truth' (1992).

19 See Feyerabend's 'Problems of Empiricism' (1965b), p. 219.

20 This holds especially for 'Problems of Empiricism' (1965b), *Against Method* (1975, 1988, 1993) and *Naturphilosophie* (2009).

21 See Feyerabend's 'Reply to Criticism. Comments on Smart, Sellars and Putnam' (1965a), pp. 224–5.

22 See for example, Feyerabend's 'Outline of a Pluralistic Theory of Knowledge and Action' (1969b).

23 Singing, performance and theatre were all lifelong interests that directly contributed to his philosophy, both in theory and practice. In 1946 he had a fellowship to study singing and stage-management for a year in Weimar at the *Musikhochschule* and he took classes in Italian, harmony, piano, singing and enunciation at the Weimar academy. He also studied theatre at the *Institut zur Methodologischen Erneuerung des Deutschen Theaters*. In 1948, he played a small part in the film *Der Prozess* directed by G. W. Pabst. In 1949, Feyerabend met Bertolt Brecht, and was offered the opportunity to become one of his production assistants. Feyerabend turned the offer

down, later describing this decision as one of his biggest mistakes of his life. But he eventually changed his mind about this, concluding that he would not have liked participating in the group surrounding Brecht. In 1952, he turned down Karl Popper's offer of an assistanceship in the philosophy of science at the prestigious London School of Economics, partly because he wanted to foster a career in professional opera singing in Vienna. Lessons from his experience with performance and the theatre were directly incorporated into his pluralistic philosophy from earlier papers through to this final performance. See for example his 'The Theatre as an Instrument of the Criticism of Ideologies: Notes on Ionesco' (1967), and his 'Let's Make More Movies' (1975), where he suggests that performance is better suited to philosophy than essays and lectures. He also used and commented extensively on dialogue as a form of philosophy, as for example in his 'Dialogue on Method' (1979) and his *Three Dialogues on Knowledge* (1991).

24 See especially his *Wissenschaft als Kunst* (1984).

1 CONFLICT AND HARMONY

1 George Gamov (1904–68) was a Russian-American theoretical physicist and cosmologist. He worked on radioactive decay of atomic nucleus, genetics and cosmic microwave background. His predictions in Big Bang cosmology were confirmed by the serendipitous discovery of the cosmic microwave background by Arno Allan Penzias and Robert Woodrow Wilson, which earned them the Nobel Prize in Physics (split with Pyotr Leonidovich Kapitsa) in 1978.

2 In 1989, NASA launched the 'Cosmic Background Explorer' (COBE) satellite to study microwave and infra-red background. In April 1992, the COBE detection empirically confirmed the Big Bang in cosmology.

3 George H. W. Bush was president during the Rodney King riots. At the time of these lectures, there were still soldiers deployed in some areas.

4 The Yugoslav Wars (1991–5) are infamous for the war crimes that took place, including ethnic cleansing, and for being the deadliest conflict in Europe since the Second World War.

5   Feyerabend is speaking from first-hand experience. He was a decorated combat veteran, having won the Iron Cross; see his autobiography, *Killing Time* (1995), ch. 4.

6   Jacques Lucien Monod (1910–76) was a French biologist. He jointly won the Nobel Prize in Physiology or Medicine together with François Jacob and André Lwoff in 1965 for discoveries concerning the genetic control of enzyme and virus synthesis.

7   Steven Weinberg (born 1933) is a prominent American physicist. He jointly won the Nobel Prize in Physics together with Abdus Salam and Sheldon Glashow in 1979 for contributing to the theory of the unified weak and electromagnetic interaction between elementary particles, including, the prediction of the weak neutral current. The paraphrase is from his *The First Three Minutes*: 'The more the universe seems comprehensible, the more it also seems pointless' (1993, p. 154).

8   Wolfgang Ernst Pauli (1900–58) was an Austrian theoretical physicist. He won the Nobel Prize in Physics in 1945 for discovering the quantum mechanical Exclusion (or 'Pauli') Principle.

9   Max Planck (1858–1947) was a German physicist. He won the Nobel Prize in Physics in 1921 in recognition of his advancement of physics by his discovery of energy quanta.

10 *Hoi polloi* is Ancient Greek for 'many' or 'majority', now used to mean 'the masses' or 'the people'.

11 See William Guthrie, *History of Greek Philosophy, Vol. I, The Earlier Presocratics and the Pythagoreans* (1962), ch. 3, section B.

12 See Umberto Eco, *The Name of the Rose* (1983). The novel evolves around a mysterious series of murders in a Benedictine monastery in Northern Italy. The murders were hiding a copy of Aristotle's *Poetics*, Book II, on comedy.

13 See Bertold Brecht, *Brecht on Theatre* (1964), p. 46.

2   THE DISUNITY OF SCIENCE

1   Jacques Monod, *Chance and Necessity* (1972), p. 170.

2   Hermann Weyl, *Philosophy of Mathematics and Natural Science* (1949), p. 116.

3   Albert Einstein, *Correspondance avec Michele Besso 1903–1955*(1979), p. 312, see also p. 292.

4   Paraphrase from Aristotle, *Metaphysica* VI 2, 1027 a19–26.

5   In a famous letter to the Grand Duchess Christina (1615), Galileo wrote: 'Nature ... is inexorable and immutable; she never transgresses the laws imposed upon her, or cares a whit whether the abstruse reasons and methods of operation are understandable to men.'

6   Leibniz wrote: 'God Almighty wants to wind up his watch from time to time: otherwise it would cease to move. He had not, it seems, sufficient foresight to make it a perpetual motion.' In H. G. Alexander (ed.) *The Leibniz–Clarke Correspondence* (1998), p. 11.

7   Paraphrase from Daniel E. Koshland, 'Sequences and Consequences of the Human Genome' (1989), p. 189.

8   The Superconducting Super Collider was a particle accelerator complex planned near Waxahachie, Texas. The project was cancelled in 1993.

9   Leonardo Olschki (1885–1961) was a German-Italian romance philologist and scholar of medieval and renaissance texts.

10   Morris Ginsberg (1889–1970) was a British sociologist. He chartered and analysed the diversity of morals among societies, between groups and individuals.

11   From 1980 to 1990, Feyerabend taught both at the University of California, Berkeley and the *Eidgenössische Technische Hochschule*, Zurich.

12   At the time of these lectures, Pope John Paul II, born Karol Józef Wojtyła, (1920-2005) held the Papacy (1978–2005).

13   Viktor Ambarzumyan [Hambardzumyan] (1908–96) was an Armenian theoretical physicist and philosopher. Halton Arp (born 1927) is an American astronomer. He is well known for his opposition to the Big Bang in cosmology.

3   THE ABUNDANCE OF NATURE

1   Ian Hacking, *Representing and Intervening* (1983).

2   Nancy Cartwright, *How the Laws of Physics Lie* (1983).

3   John Theodore Merz (1840–1922) was a British industrial chemist, historian and philosopher. Feyerabend refers to his *A History of European Thought in the Nineteenth Century*

(1907–14), which surveys scientific and philosophical thought in Germany, Britain and France.

4   Karl Ludwig Reinhardt (1886–1958) was a German classical scholar. Feyerabend refers to his *Parmenides und die Geschichte der griechischen Philosophie* (1916).

5   See William Guthrie, *History of Greek Philosophy, Vol. I, The Earlier Presocratics and the Pythagoreans* (1962), ch. 6, section 5.

6   Mircea Eliade (1907–86) was a Romanian historian of religion and philosopher. Feyerabend refers to his 4-volume work *Geschichte der religiösen Ideen, Vol. II*, (1979), p. 407. Translated into English as *History of Religious Ideas, Volume 2: From Gautama Buddha to the Triumph of Christianity* (1985).

7   Karl Popper, *Auf der Suche nach einer besseren Welt* (1984), p. 218. Translated into English as *In Search of a Better World* (1994), p. 192.

8   Czesław Miłosz (1911–2004) was a Polish poet and translator. He won the Nobel Prize in Literature in 1980. The poem '*Incantation*' was written in Berkeley in 1968; see *New and Collected Poems* (2001), p. 239.

9   Jean Améry (1912–78) was an Austrian essayist who was captured and spent several years in concentration camps during the Second World War; see for example, *At the Mind's Limits* (1980).

10 Noel Joseph Terence Montgomery Needham (1900–95) was a British biochemist and sinologist. Feyerabend refers to his *Science and Civilization in China* (1954).

11 Abraham Seidenberg (1916–88) was an American mathematician and historian of mathematics; see his 'Peg and Cord in the Ancient Greek Geometry' (1959), pp. 107–22.

4   DEHUMANIZING HUMANS

1   Erwin Friedrich Maximilian Piscator (1893–1966) was a German theatre director and producer. He was an exponent of epic theatre, along with his friend Bertold Brecht.

2   Michael Polanyi (1891–1976) was a Hungarian-British physical chemist and philosopher of science; see, for example, his *Personal Knowledge* (1958), Part II.

3   Wilhelm Heinrich Walter Baade (1893–1960) was a German astronomer. He worked at the Mount Wilson Observatory from 1931 to 1958.
4   See Eugene Ferguson, *Engineering and the Mind's Eye* (1992).
5   See Tom Wolfe, *The Bonfire of the Vanities* (1987).
6   Feyerabend refers to Cennini's *Il libro dell'arte* (*The Craftsman's Handbook*), written in the early fifteenth century.
7   Feyerabend refers to Alberti's *De Pictura* (1435).

Bibliography

Works by Paul Feyerabend

(1951). 'Zur Theorie der Basissätze'. Universität Wien, Dissertation, <http://www.univie.ac.at/ubwdb/data/nkn/m001/z024/h020/d0231979.gif>

(1955). 'Review of *Philosophical Investigations*. By Ludwig Wittgenstein', *Philosophical Review*, 64: 3, 449–83.

(1961). 'Niels Bohr's Interpretation of the Quantum Theory' in H. Feigl and G. Maxwell (eds), *Current Issues in the Philosophy of Science. Symposia of Scientists and Philosophers. Proceedings of Section L of the American Association for the Advancement of Science, 1959* (New York : Holt, Rinehart and Winston), pp. 371–90.

(1963). 'How to Be a Good Empiricist: A Plea for Tolerance in Matters Epistemological' in B. Baumrin (ed.), *Philosophy of Science: The Delaware Seminar*, Vol. II (New York: Interscience Press), pp. 3–39.

(1965a). 'Reply to Criticism. Comments on Smart, Sellars and Putnam' in R. Cohen and M. Wartofsky (eds), *Proceedings of the Boston Colloquium for the Philosophy of Science 1962–64: In Honor of Philipp Frank, Boston Studies in the Philosophy of Science*, Vol. II (New York: Humanities Press), pp. 223–61.

(1965b). 'Problems of Empiricism', in R. Colodny (ed.), *Beyond the Edge of Certainty. Essays in Contemporary Science and Philosophy* (Pittsburgh: CPS Publications in the Philosophy of Science), pp. 145–260.

Bibliography

(1967). 'The Theatre as an Instrument of the Criticism of Ideologies: Notes on Ionesco', *Inquiry*, 10: 3, 298–312.

(1968). 'On a Recent Critique of Complementarity: Part I', *Philosophy of Science*, 35: 4, 309–31.

(1969a). 'On a Recent Critique of Complementarity: Part II', *Philosophy of Science*, 36: 1, 82–105.

(1969b). 'Outline of a Pluralistic Theory of Knowledge and Action', S. Anderson (ed.), *Planning for Diversity and Choice*, (Cambridge: MIT Press), pp. 275–84.

(1970). 'Against Method: Outline of an Anarchistic Theory of Knowledge' in M. Radner and S. Winokur (eds), *Analysis of Theories and Methods of Physics and Psychology*, *Minnesota Studies in the Philosophy of Science*, Vol. IV (Minneapolis: University of Minnesota Press), pp. 17–130.

(1975, 1988, 1993, 2010). *Against Method. Outline of an Anarchistic Theory of Knowledge*, (London: New Left Books. 2nd revised edn Verso (1988). 3rd revised edn Verso (1993). 4th edn Verso (2010).

(1975). 'Let's Make More Movies' in C. Bontempo and S. Odell (eds), *The Owl of Minerva* (New York: McGraw Hill), pp. 201–10.

(1978). 'From Incompetent Professionalism to Professionalized Incompetence – The Rise of a New Breed of Intellectuals', *Philosophy of the Social Sciences*, 8: 1, 37–53.

(1979). 'Dialogue on Method' in G. Radnitzky and G. Andersson (eds), *The Structure and Development of Science* (Dordrecht: D. Reidel Pub. Co.), pp. 63–131.

(1981a). *Realism, Rationalism and Scientific Method: Philosophical Papers*, Vol. 1 (Cambridge: Cambridge University Press).

(1981b). *Problems of Empiricism: Philosophical Papers*, Vol. 2 (Cambridge: Cambridge University Press).

(1984). *Wissenschaft als Kunst* (Frankfurt am Main: Suhrkamp).

(1985). 'Galileo – The Tyranny of Truth' in G. V. Coyne, M. Heller and J. Życiński (eds), *The Galileo Affair: A Meeting of Faith and Science. Proceedings of the Cracow Conference, May 24–27, 1984* (Vatican City: Specola Vaticana), pp. 155–66.

(1987). *Farewell to Reason* (London: Verso/New Left Books, 1987).

(1991). *Three Dialogues on Knowledge* (Oxford: Blackwell).

(1992). 'Ethics as a Measure of Scientific Truth' in W. Shea and A. Spadafora (eds), *From the Twilight of Probability: Ethics and Politics* (Canton MA: Science History Publications), pp. 106–14.

(1995). *Killing Time* (Chicago: Chicago University Press).

Bibliography

(1999). *Conquest of Abundance* (Chicago: Chicago University Press).

(1999). *Knowledge, Science and Relativism: Philosophical Papers*, Vol. 3 (Cambridge: Cambridge University Press).

(2009). *Naturphilosophie* (Frankfurt am Main: Suhrkamp). English translation (Polity) is forthcoming.

Other Works

Alexander, H. G. (ed.) (1998) *The Leibniz–Clarke Correspondence* (Manchester: Manchester University Press).

Améry, Jean (1980). *At the Mind's Limits: Contemplations by a Survivor on Auschwitz and its Realities* (Bloomington: Indiana University Press).

Brecht, Bertold (1964). *Brecht on Theatre: The Development of an Aesthetic*, edited by John Willett (New York: Hill and Wang).

Cartwright, Nancy (1983). *How the Laws of Physics Lie* (Oxford: Oxford University Press).

Eco, Umberto (1983). *The Name of the Rose* (Orlando: Harcourt, Brace and Jovanovich).

Einstein, Albert (1972). *Correspondance avec Michele Besso 1903–1955* (Paris: Hermann).

Eliade, Mircea (1985). *Geschichte der religiösen Ideen*, Vol. II, Freiburg: Herder, 1979. English translation: *History of Religious Ideas, Volume 2: From Gautama Buddha to the Triumph of Christianity* (University of Chicago Press, Chicago).

Ferguson, Eugene (1992). *Engineering and the Mind's Eye* (Cambridge: MIT Press).

Guthrie, W. K. C. (1962–81). *A History of Greek Philosophy*, 6 vols (Cambridge: Cambridge University Press).

Hacking, Ian (1983). *Representing and Intervening. Introductory Topics in the Philosophy of Natural Science* (Cambridge: Cambridge University Press).

Hoyiningen-Huene (ed.) (1995). 'Two Letters of Paul Feyerabend to Thomas S. Kuhn on a Draft of *The Structure of Scientific Revolutions*', *Studies in History and Philosophy of Science*, 26: 3, 353–87.

——(ed.) (2006). 'More Letters by Paul Feyerabend to Thomas S. Kuhn on *Proto-Structure*', *Studies in History and Philosophy of Science*, 37: 4, 610–32.

Bibliography

Koshland, Daniel E. (1989). 'Sequences and Consequences of the Human Genome', *Science*, 246: 189.

Kuhn, Thomas (1962/70). *The Structure of Scientific Revolutions* (Chicago: Chicago University Press).

Merz, John Theodore (1907–14). *A History of European Thought in the Nineteenth Century*, 4 vols (Edinburgh and London: William Blackwood and Sons).

Miłosz, Czesław (2001). *New and Collected Poems, 1931–2001* (New York: Ecco).

Monod, Jacques (1972). *Chance and Necessity. An essay on the Natural Philosophy of Modern Biology* (New York: Vintage Books).

Needham, Joseph F. R. S. (1954–2004). *Science and Civilization in China*, 7 vols (Cambridge: Cambridge University Press).

Polanyi, Michael (1958). *Personal Knowledge: Towards a Post-Critical Philosophy* (Chicago: University of Chicago Press).

Popper, Karl (1994). *Auf der Suche nach einer besseren Welt* (Munich: Piper, 1984). English translation: *In Search of a Better World: Lectures and Essays from Thirty Years* (London: Routledge).

Preston, John (1998). 'Science as Supermarket: "Post-Modern" Themes in Paul Feyerabend's Later Philosophy of Science', *Studies in History and Philosophy of Science*, 29: 3, 425–47.

——(2009). 'Paul Feyerabend' in Edward N. Zalta (ed.), *Stanford Encyclopaedia of Philosophy* (Winter 2009 Edn) <http://plato.stanford.edu/archives/win2009/entries/feyerabend/>.

Preston, J., Munévar, G. and Lamb, D. (eds) (2000). *The Worst Enemy of Science? Essays in Memory of Paul Feyerabend* (New York: Oxford University Press).

Reinhardt, Karl Ludwig (1916). *Parmenides und die Geschichte der griechischen Philosophie* (Bonn: Verlag von Friedrich Cohen).

Seidenberg, Abraham (1959). 'Peg and Cord in the Ancient Greek Geometry', *Scripta Mathematica*, 24:107–22.

Theocharis, T. and M. Psimopoulos (1987). 'Where Science has Gone Wrong', *Nature*, 329: 6140, 595–8.

Weinberg, Steven (1993). *The First Three Minutes. A Modern View of the Origin of the Universe* 2nd edn (New York: Basic Books).

Weyl, Hermann (1949). *Philosophy of Mathematics and Natural Science*, Princeton: Princeton University Press.

Wolfe, Tom (1987). *The Bonfire of the Vanities* (New York: Bantam Books).

146

Index

Index

Index

Index